SELECTED AND

NEW POEMS

The Horsehair Sofa

Prayers of the North American Martyrs

Alehouse Sonnets

In the Dead of the Night

The Illustrations

A Thousand Little Things

The City of the Olesha Fruit

Odalisque in White

Popham of the New Song

The Everlastings

The Window in the Field

SELECTED

AND

NEW POEMS

Norman Dubie

W · W · NORTON & COMPANY

New York   *London*

Citations are due to the following periodicals in which new poems
in this book first appeared: *The American Poetry Review:* "At Mid-
summer," "Chemin de Fer," "Elegy for Wright & Hugo"; *The
Georgia Review:* "Elsinore in the Late Ancient Autumn"; *The Gra-
mercy Review:* "Penelope"; *The New Yorker:* "An Old Woman's
Vision," "Parish," "To a Young Woman Dying at Weir," copy-
right © 1982, 1981, 1980 by The New Yorker Magazine, Inc.,
reprinted by permission; *Ploughshares:* "Grandmother"; *Poetry:*
"Pictures at an Exhibition," "Revelations"; *Porch:* "Several Mea-
sures for the Little Lost."

Poems from *The Illustrations* were originally published by George
Braziller, and the author wishes to thank that press for permission
to include poems from that volume. A special thanks to Kathleen
Anderson.

The text of this book is composed in Electra, with display type set
in Bembo. Composition and manufacturing by The Maple-Vail
Book Manufacturing Group. Book design by Christine Aulicino.

FIRST EDITION

Library of Congress Cataloging in Publication Data
Dubie, Norman, 1945–
Selected and new poems.
I. Title.
PS3554.U255A6   1983   811'.54   83–8046

ISBN 0-393-01817-2

ISBN 0-393-30140-0 (pbk.)

W. W. Norton & Company, Inc.,
500 Fifth Avenue, New York, N.Y. 10110
W. W. Norton & Company Ltd.,
37 Great Russell Street, London WC1B 3NU

1 2 3 4 5 6 7 8 9 0

For Jeannine and Hannah

and

For My Parents

CONTENTS

III. THE CITY OF THE OLESHA FRUIT

IV. THE EVERLASTINGS

V. NEW POEMS

I

IN THE DEAD

OF THE NIGHT

FOR RANDALL JARRELL, 1914–1965

What the wish wants to see, it sees.

All the dead are eating little yellow peas
Off knives under the wing of an owl
While the living run around, not aimlessly, but
Like two women in white dresses gathering
Hymnbooks out on a lawn with the first
Drops of rain already falling on them.

Once, I wrote a sudden and enormous sentence
At the bottom of a page in a notebook
Next to a sketch of a frog. The sentence
Described the gills of a sunfish
As being the color of cut rhubarb, or
Of basil if it is dried in a bundle
In a red kitchen with the last winter light
Showing it off, almost purple.

Anything approaching us we try to understand, say,
Like a lamp being carried up a lane at midnight.

Jeremy Taylor knew it watching an orange leaf
Go down a stream.
Self-taught, it came to us, I believe,
As old age to a panther who's about to
Spring from one branch to another but suddenly
Thinks better of it.
She says to us from her tree:
"Please, one world at a time!" and leaps—

Making it, which could mean,
Into this world or some other. And between.

NEW ENGLAND, COMPLINE

A dark, thick branch in the last light is like
The hand of your grandmother
Dropping linen napkins on the shrubs to dry
Hopelessly in the few hours before night.
Across the garden
In the back a girl strikes a piano key just once
And then there is the sound of crickets. The evening

Itself seems slow with the oldest feelings:
A boy walks up the hill
With a glass jar; inside he has, perhaps, a snake,
A firefly or minnows. Three houses away
A man standing on his roof passes a short ladder
Down to his wife.

The stone nude beside the garden is bathing
In deep shade while inside the mouth
Of the nude in a copper dish a sparrow washes
Both its wings.

In the dark there's a last sound, it is
A large jar breaking in the street, and up into the night
Almost heavy
Go fireflies striking their soft, yellow lights.

THE PENNACESSE LEPER COLONY FOR WOMEN, CAPE COD: 1922

The island, you mustn't say, had only rocks and scrub pine;
Was on a blue, bright day like a blemish in this landscape.
And Charolette who is frail and the youngest of us collects
Sticks and branches to start our fires, cries as they burn
Because they resemble most what she has lost
Or has little of: long fingers, her toes
And a left arm gone past the elbow, soon clear to her shoulder.
She has the mouth of sea perch. Five of our sisters wear
Green hoods. You are touched by all of this, *but not by us.*
To be touched by us; to be kissed! Sometimes
We see couples rowing in the distance in yellow coats.

Sometimes they fish with handlines; we offend
Everyone who are offended most
By everything and everyone. The five goats love us, though,
And live in our dark houses. When they are
Full with milk they climb the steps and beg that
They be milked. Their teats brush the steps and leave thick
Yellow trails of fresh milk. We are all females here.
Even the ghosts. We must wash, of course, in saltwater
But it smarts or maybe it even hurts us. Often with a rope
Around her waist Anne is lowered entirely into the water.
She splashes around and screams in pain. Her screams
Sometimes carry clear to the beaches on the Cape.

For us I say so often. For us we say. *For us!* We are
Human and not individual, we hold everything in common.
We are individual, you could pick us out in a crowd.
You did. This island is not our prison. We are not kept
In; not even by our skin.

Once Anne said she would love to be a negro or a trout.

We live without you. Father, I don't know why I have written
You this; but be proud for I am living, and yet each day
I am less and less your flesh. Someday, eventually, you
Should only think of me as being a lightning bug on the lawn,
Or the negro fishing at the pond, or the fat trout he wraps
In leaves that he is showing to someone. I'll be

Most everything for you. And I'll be gone.

PASTORAL

It happened so fast. Fenya was in the straight
Chair in the corner, her youngest sucking
On her breast. The screams, and a horseman
Outside the cottage. Then, her father in a blue tunic
Falling through the door onto the boards.
Fenya leaned over him, her blouse
Still at the waist and a single drop of her yellow milk
Falling into the open eye of her father. He dies
Looking up through this screen, what he sees

Is a little lamp-glow,
Like the poet describes less often even than harness bells
Or the icon with pine boughs. He sees snow
Falling into a bland field where a horse is giving
Birth to more snow dragging its placenta all over
The glaze which is red; all the snow is red, the horse's
Blood is white. He sees tears on Fenya's face and
Milk coming like bone hairpins from her breasts.
The straight force in the twig that makes a great black
Branch. Two of which are crossed over his chest. Terror is

The vigil of astonishment.

THE OBSCURE

It's the poor first light of morning.

The woman still sleeps in her unheated room.
The man in his nightshirt stands
In the kitchen burning
Dry sunflower stalks in the open stove.
There's not a single lamp working.
The orange light from the stove
Shows just the things in the far corner.

Outside the window it is still snowing.

The harvest is finished. The time has come
For killing the pig.
They have been starving him for a week;
Yesterday, emptying him completely
With a wet portion of barley meal.
The pig is hungry and squeals in his corner
By the garden.

The man has dressed in an old canvas coat.
He stands inside the branch fence
Beside the sty, and with a broom sweeps
A clearing in the snow.
He lays out the knives, the rope,
And a black stool.

Birds stream from the tree above him.

The pig is stuck in the windpipe, he hangs
By the rope from the tree, and upside down
Spins slowly above the stool,
His eyes never leave this man
Who brought him so many warm vegetables.

The man's thoughts never leave the woman
Who is still sleeping up in the house.
She walked through the woods in the snow
For most of the evening. For the second night
In their lives she wouldn't be touched
By him.

The pig is ready for scalding. He has
Never before been this heated and pink.
A high window opens in the house. Icicles fall
From the windowsill. The woman looks out
Opening her eyes to the bright snow:
The pig hangs in the tree like an ornament of wax
Stuck with a few red jewels, she had not
Been warned about the killing;
There's her scream and then
Just a silence leaving the man to himself,

To little else but the thought
That her breasts filled the window like a mouth.

ABOUT INFINITY

There are stone breakers in straw hats
Drinking from jars under a shade tree.
You are dressed all in white like the clematis
And look down into a meadow where your father
Is working on a watercolor of two silver trees.
The two trees are parallel.
He looks back at you:
You are wishing he hadn't died making with
His chest a sound like cows running in a stream.

Cows eat the flowers, they eat off the trees;
And the seed packets of the milk-white clematis
Have no turnings: they sit, almost purple,
In steady needles that are vertical, North
And South, repeating abstractly
That such parallel things must meet
Somewhere in a limitless glut of peace.

There are men in straw hats drinking from clear
Jars of water.
There are two silver trees whose pink roots
Will meet, not abstractly, but under the meadow
Where for minerals and the water
They mean to kill one another. There are cows

Running in a running stream.

ANIMA POETA: A CHRISTMAS ENTRY
FOR THE SUICIDE, MAYAKOVSKY

It has nothing to do with the warmth of moonset
If I say to you
The cities are prose, or that my daughter
Is growing more beautiful than
Before when her hair was white and cut short.
The first Wednesday after the peace
With Germany was like a new brook
Under the rain, which only the rain could make.

You dream of a steamer with a clean pine cabin.
The fog in the wreaths.
The bullets were chalk-white larvae
That slept in the chambers
Of a revolver you left near the door;
Larvae, a Latin word for ghosts,
The pieces of iron letting go
Of their little red hammer and its stirrup
Sending you a visitor,
The moth that dips inside your head: you were
Gone before you hit the boards on the floor.

Think of yourself with your black fingers
In the flowerpots, in the candlelight,
The double violets and scarlet Anthus
Of a narrow window.
You were trying
To remember the French word
For a hedgerow sparrow that soldiers
Made captive for its song. You thought
The kingfisher
Was so slow when in the vicinity of winter
That even a bureaucrat
Would distinguish all its colors. Mayakovsky,

You watched a snail one afternoon eat twice
Its length in brooklime.
When you were young

You could list all the birds of passage,
Much later in your life you joined them.

MONOLOGUE OF TWO MOONS, NUDES
WITH CRESTS: 1938

Once, Lily and I fell from a ladder
And startled the white geese that were
Concealed in the shadows of the house, and
I wrote much later that the geese
Broke from the shadows like handkerchiefs
Out of the sleeves of black dresses

At a burial. When the matron was sick
It was work to carry the powders
On blue paper and the clear water
With a spoon into her large, cold room.

In the evenings we would look out
At the spruce trees. It was wrong to have
Visitors. It was wrong those clear nights
To remember that boys were out on the hills
Falling onto sleds or into their gray baskets.

We were two young girls with black hair
And the white cones
Of our breasts, Lily said, "I will put
My hand, here, on you and follow the rib, and
You can put your hand, here, on me,
Up the inside of my leg."
We spent that Christmas morning pressing
Satin skirts for the boys' choir. We take
Butter away from the closet.
We take the lamp away from the green
Cadaverous child who is not ours.

I have a little violin pupil who eats
Bread in cream.

.Ve love the details mice leave in flour.
The way the clouds
Are low before a storm in early summer.

Lily slept with a Jew once in Vienna.
I opened my hand that morning
On a milk jug that had frozen and cracked
On the doorstep.
Yesterday, I saw the perfect impression
Of a bee in asphalt. It was under a shade tree.
Lily said, "I will kiss in the morning
Your mouth which will be red and thick
After sleep." She has left me
For a banker she met in the gardens.
The gas jets are on: they are
Like fountains of the best water. I am

Remembering the vertical action of two birds
Building a nest. It's in Munich and
Both birds are dark and crested,
But the female, I think, is the one whose
Nesting materials are wet things:

Twigs, leaves, and an infinite black string.

ELEGY ASKING THAT IT BE THE LAST

(For Ingrid Erhardt, 1951–1971)

There's a bird the color of mustard. The bird
Is held in a black glove. This bird
Has a worm in its heart.
Inside the heart of the worm there's
A green passage of blood.
The bird is a linnet.
The glove is worn by a Prince. There's a horse
Under him. It is another century: things are
Not better or worse. The horse is chestnut,
The horse
Is moving its bowels while standing in the surf.
The cliffs behind him are dark. It is
The coast of Scotland. It's winter.
Surrounding the Prince and also on horses are men
Who are giant; they are dressed in furs.
There's ice forming in their beards. Each is
A chieftain. They are the Prince's heavy protection.
They are drunk, these men who are laughing
At the linnet with a worm in its heart.
This is a world set apart from ours. It is not!

I I

THE

ILLUSTRATIONS

NINETEEN FORTY

They got Lewes at last yesterday.
—Virginia Woolf

The sun just drops down through the poplars.

I should sit out and watch it rather than
Write this!

The red of it sweeps along the houses past the marsh
To where L. is picking apples.
The air is cold.
Little things seem large.
Behind me there's moisture like windows on the pears.

And then the planes going to London. Well, it's
An hour before that yet. There are cows eating grass.
There were bombs dropped on Itford Hill. Yesterday,
I watched a Messerschmitt smudge out in the sky.

What is it like when the bone-shade is crushed in
On your eye. You drain. And pant. And, then, dot, dot, dot!

Walking Sunday (Natalie's birthday) by Kingfisher Pool
I saw my first hospital train. It was slow but not laden,
Not like a black shoebox but like a weight pulled by
A string. And bone-shaking!
Private and heavy it cut through the yellow fields:

And a young airman with his head in his hands,
With his head in a fat, soiled bandage, moved
His good eye, and nothing else, up to the high corner
Of his window and through the cool, tinted glass watched,

I believe, as
Individual wild ducks scraped and screamed in along a marsh.

FEBRUARY: THE BOY BREUGHEL

The birches stand in their beggar's row:
Each poor tree
Has had its wrists nearly
Torn from the clear sleeves of bone,
These icy trees
Are hanging by their thumbs
Under a sun
That will begin to heal them soon,
Each will climb out
Of its own blue, oval mouth;
The river groans,
Two birds call out from the woods

And a fox crosses through snow
Down a hill; then, he runs,
He has overcome something white
Beside a white bush, he shakes
It twice, and as he turns
For the woods, the blood in the snow

Looks like the red fox,
At a distance, running down the hill:
A white rabbit in his mouth killed
By the fox in snow
Is killed over and over as just
Two colors, now, on a winter hill:

Two colors! Red and white. A barber's bowl!
Two colors like the peppers
In the windows
Of the town below the hill. Smoke comes
From the chimneys. Everything is still.

Ice in the river begins to move,
And a boy in a red shirt who woke
A moment ago
Watches from his window
The street where an ox
Who's broken out of his hut
Stands in the fresh snow
Staring cross-eyed at the boy
Who smiles and looks out
Across the roof to the hill;
And the sun is reaching down
Into the woods

Where the smoky red fox still
Eats his kill. Two colors.
Just two colors!
A sunrise. The snow.

THE CZAR'S LAST CHRISTMAS LETTER:
A BARN IN THE URALS

You were never told, Mother, how old Illya was drunk
That last holiday, for five days and nights

He stumbled through Petersburg forming
A choir of mutes, he dressed them in pink ascension gowns

And, then, sold Father's Tirietz stallion so to rent
A hall for his Christmas recital: the audience

Was rowdy but Illya in his black robes turned on them
And gave them that look of his; the hall fell silent

And violently he threw his hair to the side and up
Went the baton, the recital ended exactly one hour

Later when Illya suddenly turned and bowed
And his mutes bowed, and what applause and hollering

Followed.
All of his cronies were there!

Illya told us later that he thought the voices
Of mutes combine in a sound

Like wind passing through big, winter pines.
Mother, if for no other reason I regret the war

With Japan for, you must now be told,
It took the servant, Illya, from us. *It was confirmed.*

He would sit on the rocks by the water and with his stiletto
Open clams and pop the raw meats into his mouth

And drool and laugh at us children.
We hear guns often, now, down near the village.

Don't think me a coward, Mother, but it is comfortable
Now that I am no longer Czar. I can take pleasure

From just a cup of clear water. I hear Illya's choir often.
I teach the children about decreasing fractions, that is

A lesson best taught by the father.
Alexandra conducts the French and singing lessons.

Mother, we are again a physical couple.
I brush out her hair for her at night.

She thinks that we'll be rowing outside Geneva
By the spring. I hope she won't be disappointed.

Yesterday morning while bread was frying
In one corner, she in another washed all'of her legs

Right in front of the children. I think
We became sad at her beauty. She has a purple bruise

On an ankle.
Like Illya I made her chew on mint.

Our Christmas will be in this excellent barn.
The guards flirt with your granddaughters and I see . . .

I see nothing wrong with it. Your little one, who is
Now a woman, made one soldier pose for her, she did

Him in charcoal, but as a bold nude. He was
Such an obvious virgin about it; he was wonderful!

Today, that same young man found us an enormous azure
And pearl samovar. Once, he called me Great Father

And got confused.
He refused to let me touch him.

I know they keep your letters from us. But, Mother,
The day they finally put them in my hands

I'll know that possessing them I am condemned
And possibly even my wife, and my children.

We will drink mint tea this evening.
Will each of us be increased by death?

With fractions as the bottom integer gets bigger, Mother, it
Represents less. That's the feeling I have about

This letter. I am at your request, The Czar.
And I am Nicholas.

THESE UNTITLED LITTLE VERSES IN WHICH, AT DAWN, TWO OBSCURE DUTCH PEASANTS STRUGGLED WITH AN AUBURN HORSE

The water is green. The two boats out at a distance
Are silver, and the two gulls coming in

Off the water are, also, silver;
But these peasants and their horse, at first light,

Seem absorbed in the pitch-blackness
Of a previous night. They are in a field

That climbs away from the sea joining
A thick row of white almond trees.

The younger of the two men holds a small branch,
The other

Holds a rope that leads away from the horse
Running over his shoulder and underneath the arm

To a pool of rope beneath him: he leans,
Or he reclines like a lever in the scene.

The auburn horse
Represents some inevitable sadness

That will visit each of us, that visits
These two peasants struggling in a winter pasture.

It is the morning.
It is dawn. These three may

Signal a common enough passage from the night
To the day. It begins like pain for the older man:

/ 2 5

It begins to rain.
The two men run to the trees just above them

And the horse, ignorant of everything, walks away
Like a skilled butcher from a dark, maimed

Lamb still wiggling in the grass behind him. And
Morning surrenders to mid-day, and the afternoon

To the evening, and the evening surrenders everything
To the sleep of these two peasants

Who have had a discouraging day in the fields:
They dream of the black, burial horses of a king

With heavy sable plumes and the blinders
Of gold-leaf made starry with diamonds,

Horses not like the auburn mare who stood
In a world that

Belongs to a system of things
Which presents a dark humus with everything

Living: all of us preceded
Not by the lovely, braided horses

Of which the peasants dreamed, but by these two
Peasants and their horse struggling

Briefly, at dawn, in the deep trenches
Of a field beside the green, winter sea.

THE IMMORALIST

Samaden, the Julier, Tiefenkasten . . . the raw egg
I broke into the harness bells, and the strong reversals
Of cold, sour wine. The marshlike waters on the other
Honeymoon were a new train, as early as Neuchatel, and
Overlooking a lake, past some cows, the first signals
Of melancholy. I didn't leave her all day.

I had heard of other cases of tuberculosis
That were much worse. And wasn't there something
I didn't know about myself? I blamed everything on
Whatever few biscuits Marceline broke
Into her soup. She coughed horribly.
Besides, what did we need money for? A winter in Engadine?
I no longer have my lectures. We are drunk and weak.

I have again made love to a woman saving blood
In her mouth. I remember the way the other sloshed
Wine around with her tongue. Her laughter.
And the reeds of a hideous black lake. The hotel
Was empty. The honest Swiss. Even their rosebushes
Told her I would push a pillow
To her face. (Hard benches by the water, and the blankets
Over her legs. I didn't leave her all day.)

From the train through glass: larches and fir,
And the crease of the pillowcase on her black cheek
Filling slowly like her grave,
Like the trench of a young couple crossing a lake.

GHOST

If a man stands by a pin oak emptying
A thermos onto the ground and it is cold
In the light, and the light itself
Has condensed
Inside his bones, would you walk up to him
And say, "I went to the clay house. It still
Smells of the hickory, even now in November.
I want to know what is going
To happen to everyone."
The sound of churchbells comes out of
The cane-brake.
The insides of three birds are smoking
On the ground by his feet. He watches

A leaf come all the way down out
Of its tree. Then he speaks, "Look, little pigeon,
What are you doing
Out here in your nightgown? Your hair
Is wet. You're standing in your bare feet
Like the girls down in the cabins.
You should have visited me earlier: I waited
For you here each evening in the summer. I covered
The bird entrails with leaves.
There was a smell of plums. The fox
Was in the clearing. Does your mother
Forgive me. I didn't mean to . . . you tell

Me 'that's lost' and 'that's dead'
And 'I don't remember ever owning a red dress.'
You know that night before I went into
The fields, as much as she had hurt me in the afternoon,
I laid down the gun
To draw water in the tub for her. She should
Find that a pleasant memory.

Tell her they were wrong. 'It could have been
An accident.'
When I went out the door the tub
Was still filling and she called to me
That she'd see to it. I have a memory of her, naked
Running to a tub as if to someone, and
Her mouth is opening. She kneels almost
Without getting near it, and, out of breath,
Just stares at the faucets for a moment; then reaches
Touching the collar of the coat. I am bleeding.
Leaves are stuck to my chest. Then, there's
A sound she hears down in the cane, and
Really it's much more
Than a sound, but not yet a noise.

It's like a tub overflowing onto a floor."

SUN AND MOON FLOWERS: PAUL KLEE, 1879–1940

First, there is the memory of the dead priest in Norway
Dressed in a straw hat, his tie that's white
But splashed with violet and the black skirt;
He'll hang forever in the deer park.
Beneath him German officers
Are weaving in and out of trees in a white sunlight.

When there is music crossing over the water from France
The little steamers pull their beds of coal
Slowly up the canal, and, Klee,
You walk back to your room saying:
"What on earth happened to us? Any simple loss
Is like the loss of all of us. Nothing's secret?
Just look straight into the North Sea.
And, then, tell me there's anything they can keep from us."

The matron who walked you through the orchard at Orsolina
Should have said: "There's a black star with conifers."
Klee, don't listen to them. Next Wednesday your heart
Stops like a toad. You're dying of a skin disease.
They are not telling you about this war, the Luftwaffe,
The Nazi who's resting on a sofa beside a stream,
And, Klee, this Nazi is inside Poland. And
In Poland your moon flowers have already begun growing!

The opaque dice in your painting can no longer
Be mistaken for some weathered houses by the coast.
The woman sick with tuberculosis says to you,
"A war will clear the air!"
The war puts priests in trees. Puts a sparrow's nest
Beside a sleeve in a train station in Tuscany.
You and your friends saw the unlikely, ruptured ceilings
And painted them; but not as premonitions, or images

Of war—
The war your family won't acknowledge or discuss
But an orderly who has news of Poland whispers
To the day nurse: she touches her blouse.
You ask her what is happening.
You make a scene. And then she says what is necessary
By slipping you a morning tray

With its ice water, blue spikes of lupine, and morphine.

IBIS

There is the long dream in the afternoon
That turns a large, white page

Like, once, the slow movement
Of slaves at daybreak

Through the clouds of a stone laundry.
The blossom

On a black vegetable and
The olive wood burning in the plate

Are the simple events
That I'll wake to this evening.

At dark, we'll walk out along
The shore having finished

Another day of exile in a wet place.
As a boy I burned

Leaves in the many gardens
Of a cemetery in Rome.

I wrote in my diary:
A blue vessel

Is filling out in the rain. All day,
Here, the water falls and is not broken,

But it punishes me like the girls
With their clubs and bowl

Flattening the new maize,
Millet, and the narrow tubers

Of yam
That are white like hill snow.

Postumius is my servant-boy, he plays
All morning in the sea.

He says, "Ovid. The red ibis flies north!"
I hate him.

He visits me between phantoms
And like them,

Like the goat, you can trace the muscles
In his leg and the purple ropes

Of blood that climb
Through his throat. At the saltmarsh

He searches for the moon snail
With its lavender egg-pouch;

He eats them after
Soaking them in brookwater . . .

Days that follow in rain
Make him nervous and he eats

Everything off the dry shelf: the individual
Oval seeds, he cracks

The winter wheat between his teeth
With a sound

Like a child working its teeth
In a bad dream.

If he stands all day in the marsh
In the sun, then, he returns to me

As a new coin. I am jealous
Of him.

He smiles at me. There are the shadows
With the olive wood burning in the plate.

It's dark. We walk out along
The shore of the Black Sea.

There's the noise of the ibis
Who raises a bleached wing in waking.

There is a boat decaying by a tree.
It's radiant

Like the shearwater birds
Standing here and there among rocks.

Postumius touches my shoulder, "Ovid?
About Rome when the moon

Was broken on the ground and the ferns
Stood against the blue-black sky?"

I do remember the bleachers in the arena
And a lion's paw raised, that erased

The face of a young Thracian.
I tell him he is a stupid boy!

We walk back
Passing the wharves and straw-houses.

I say to Postumius
That when I am dead

He must fuel the terracotta lamp
And gather the cress and hidden eggs

Of the ibis. He smiles at me, I do
Love him, at moments;

As, then, he sleeps next to me,
Never sharing the work

Of turning the page, as slowly he turns
All of his new body away from me.

THE TREES OF MADAME BLAVATSKY

There is always the cough. In the afternoon
They go out for long walks as partners,
Arms linked, woman and woman,
Man and man, woman and man. And they keep
Their feet. I can't judge if she supports
The other in green.
Perhaps, they support one another? I've
Followed them for miles and they conceal
Everything in weakness. They have
The hind legs of cows.
When horses eat fermented hay it brings up
The lining of the intestine which they
Tug at
Like gloves all the way past the elbows.

If we could follow them far enough we would
Come to their meeting place
Where they are all wired up like flowers,
They live in this camp, serene and delayed.
They are the oldest sopranos resuming
With care the phrases,
Listen, there is a song they sing at night,
The regalia inside their chests, and this song,
Which blames the memory, is wrong and not wrong
Like a girl
Showing her breasts to a boy in a cemetery.

ELEGIES FOR THE OCHRE DEER ON THE WALLS AT LASCAUX

> *This and the like together establish the realm of* IT.
>
> *"In order to come to love," says Kierkegaard about his renunciation of Regina Olsen, "I had to remove the object."*
>
> *Kierkegaard does not conceal from us for a moment that his religious doctrine of loneliness is personal. He confesses that he "ceased to have common speech" with men. He notes that the finest moment in his life is in the bathhouse, before he plunges into the water: "by then I am having nothing more to do with the world."*
>
> *—Martin Buber*

PROLOGUE

You are hearing a distant, almost familiar, French cradlesong
While drinking bottled water
Along the roadside to Copenhagen.

There are children of six who speak
In secret to imaginary friends
On summer evenings before bed.

In some old houses there are walls where there were doors.
And doors where there were windows.
And where there were once floors of broken field stones
There are, now, blue ceilings.

There is a sudden smell of roses in a room.

Once, there was a hunter
Dressed in skins, in the black and mauve summer-molt of bison,
And he would squat down before a wet, serpentine wall and make

An image. (A virgin is singing: My Lords, turn in, turn in!)

I suppose all of this means nothing to you; there's still
The blue tiles of the bathhouse floor, and the orange lamps
Burning above the moving surface of the water. A nude lawyer
Is smoking a cigar on a birch-sofa next to a lieutenant
Who's exercising in an Army blanket. You'll forget them
As you leave the edge making a little figure
In the air as you enter the steaming, blue pool:

Søren, a winter evening in the bathhouse, and just past
The surface of the water you saw
The *will* to *be!*

The *will* to *be* is, perhaps, teeth, throat,
And intestine leaving the floor of an ocean
With the slight movement of its tail. The *will* to *be* is often
Not pretty, but dorsal like the sable plumes on helmets, or

Like the man at Lascaux in his black-and-mauve skins
Who with friends stands at the edge of a pit
That holds reindeer, they shower the deer with stones,
And, then, there's a silence; our caveman

Reaches down into the pit and draws out a white fawn
Who, weak from swimming in the blood of the others, wobbles
For a moment and, then, runs off into a forest: *and, Søren,*

The fawn made bright, finite tracks through the leaves
Like your own red lettering in a diary

That believes the gods of China must be Chinese.

I. 1916

The way the mist in the mountains can circle a young fir,
A boulder or the fern and purple vetch of the timberline
Which are waving as children after a pageant

Through the mist and rain to someone seated way above them
On a rotting bench at the summit of the mountain.
It's young Theodisius, the Jesuit,

Breathing heavily
After his climb, remembering a formal procession
Up a hill in St. Louis. He looks down through the Notch:

The priest knows desire to be a comedy of place and
A surge forward as with the boy and his tuba
In this parade at St. Louis: the boy had become faint
In his blue wool suit and silver cap,
And so under the sun while descending the hill he suddenly
Went rudely through ranks of clarinets and, then,
He wrecked a section of oboes and bassoons:

Death is a descent, or the traverse that is like
A surprising destruction of music moving
With the force of a sun-struck tuba
Down a hill where, at last, our fainting musician falls
Into the arms of laughing women
Who are wearing large hats and red pantaloons.

Theodisius is romantic; he has climbed a mountain
In the mist and rain to wait, now, through the day
For a change in the weather, for the sun to burn through
And what joy he'll feel

At the ease with which individual trees
Are regained in a familiar enough
Landscape of mountains with a clear lake and ponds.

In China, Theodisius would be mistaken for an eccentric,

But a conventional Chinese wisdom has always taken
The musician in his green trout-gown for being
Eccentric as he is musical.
Theodisius' instrument was the tuba.

Yes, our Jesuit often thinks of concepts of death
When reminded of childhood embarrassments.
Theodisius is a young Jesuit who remembers
The sad little crèche in Bethlehem.

He is now waiting for the sun to burn away the mist
In the mountains: *the beer gardens of St. Louis were often
Like this. Anyway,*

The fern and purple vetch are waving to the young priest
Who leaves his wet bench like Odysseus climbing up
Out of the surf: it's early morning,
He stares to the East where he thinks the sun will soon
Break everything wide open:

Theodisius, our poor Theodisius, still stands in mist.

He studies the cascades and a flaw in an icy waterfall,
He remembers
How his mother each spring boiled her best crystal chandelier
Through the long hours of the afternoon into evening.
Theodisius believes that beyond all doubt he is dangerous
To himself.

There have been many changes in him, and none
In the weather: he remembers
His mother's playing cards that were perfumed with balsam,
And how confidently she flicked them out singly

Over the table, how the young men seated
At the table could not remove their eyes
From her quick hands or her exposed bosom just beyond them.

Once crossing a stream with her, here, in these mountains
She lifted her skirts like the women in the lithograph
Of a circus at Trieste,
And Theodisius, a boy of twelve, went face first
Into the water, his mother laughing as she joined him:

They are both laughing now as they embrace,
Suspended, not quite seated on the stream bed.
Theodisius thought all the colors of that lithograph
Were there in that water. He forgets,

And looks down into the spruce and aspen.
He spots several deer along the edges of a clearing.
He approaches them like a man
Falling through crust in a snowfield.
He is still thinking of his mother; this time, as she leans
Smiling over a balcony beside a white tree.
He thought the skin of the deer seemed shaded
As with lichen. The deer knew he was weak.
But they clattered off over the stone surface of the clearing
Into the mist and leaves.
Theodisius looked away from them to the running stream
With its small delays: the silver archipelagoes,

Pools and blue basins.
He remembered Greek girls dancing in the beer gardens
Of St. Louis.

Deserted even by the gentle deer, Theodisius

Became monumental and literal: he believed
He was the breeze tipping a wet bough of a tree, a breeze
Created by the passing of a red caboose pulled along swiftly
Over a mountain trellis,

A mountain trellis which stands in the sudden sunlight
Just beneath him, the mountain trellis
From which he hangs by the neck like the pastel daredevil
At Trieste in a famous lithograph
His mother nailed to the headboard of his small bed

Just beneath a chartreuse-and-red watercolor of the dead Jesus.

1872

Isiah Potter walks solemnly from his old salt-box
And tar-shingle house onto the stone walk
And looks up the street past the roses
To the granite hitching posts. He loves the Orient.

Reverend Potter is composing a sermon
On the tragedy of green. He walks down the street
Under the elms thinking that once in a vision
He saw two men mowing in a field: there were ashes
On their shoulders and long daffodils shot through
Their necks and chests like arrows: he heard

An isolated choir up in a stand of trees
Behind the field. He woke, it was midnight
And he went down to the kitchen for bread in milk.
His father, Amos,
Had been dead for two winters. All the new moons
And sabbaths. The grief calling of women and children.
Isiah Potter killed himself by leaping
From a ledge into the lake. The village wanted
A dull lighting of his face, a green abscissa
In his memory, in the vestibule of the meeting house.
The portrait of Isiah Potter has remained
In the vestibule for a hundred years, and

The nighthawks are still crying above the ledges of the lake,
And below them on the rocks a young raccoon
Who's eaten a sunfish washes his paws
And legs; he looks up at the night sky where

Suddenly there is something like sheet lightning
Giving way to the yellow, blue, and pink parachutes
Of The Chinese Fire & Rain which is spreading out
Over the lake and dissolving back into a white light,

And, again, it's the arsenic and antimony
Of The Snow Orchard: this is fireworks

Streaming steadily, now, from two large wooden boats
That were rowed quietly to the middle of the lake.

There's the shooting sparks of The Blue Fox.
The Snow Orchard, again, but mixed with two rockets
Of gold Cassandra Buttons, and, then, after a silence
When the frogs begin once more with their groaning:
There's the explosion of a loud, red Camphor Goose.

There's the smell of gunpowder. You can hear the water
Coming up against the rocks and trees along the shore.
And the spotted animals in the leaves have begun breathing.
For centuries in China the sky was painted on moonless nights;
What did the civet cats, martens, and black bear of Liaosi Lake
Do watching soldiers with torches touching
Off rockets beside an old pavillion of wet banyan leaves:

The white Calomel Fountain goes up blazing with the low fire
Of three Blue Suns, and you can make out

The terraced hillside with the tallow and yew trees,
Pine and willow, and the orange brick pagoda by a stream
Where two priests are eating melons and roots.

There was an owl in the yew tree: his eyes like twin lakes,
And the two large wooden boats are now being rowed back
To the beach where the children are letting go
Of their mothers' dresses, where watermelons
Are divided by a long, curved blade and night bathers
Are drying in the cold in the light of two fires.
A girl sits on a log

And closes her eyes wanting to see again the blues and yellows,
The falling chains of The Chinese Fire & Rain;

43

Her older sister is far up the beach past the rocks
And she is nude after swimming with a friend, he drags
A day lily over her stomach and she shuts her eyes.
She, also, sees the ghostly paper chains
Falling out of the black sky into the water. She kisses

Her friend and quickly they run into the trees,
And as with the fireworks, the image
Of their white buttocks stays behind in the mind
Of a young raccoon who's on the rocks trembling,
The dark circles around his eyes are increasingly
Larger like the circles of broken water
On the lake where a fish has just jumped for a deerfly:

This, then, was midsummer, not a new season:

It's Isiah Potter's sermon about the green tips
Of things, a green conclusion to everything.
Accept death, he says, don't fear the daffodils
That pierce your chest or the ones that are burning
As they arc through the open windows of your houses.

Isiah Potter walked solemnly from his old salt-box
And tar-shingle house onto a stone walk
And looked up the street past the roses
To the Orient. (He woke a lunatic.) It was
The Sabbath, and he worked on his sermon
As he walked toward the meetinghouse: the green things,

The judgments, and the faintings in the first garden
In the gilded book, the monotony of an animal or angel,
The couple nude beside the rocks, and

He thought: the eyes of the owl are twin, green lakes
As it glides down from its tree in China, closing, now,
On a fieldmouse where suddenly there are four rockets

Climbing: a white fountain and three blue suns burning
And the owl crumpled on the terraced hillside. Also,

He thought,
The bald heads of two priests can be seen
Like the white buttocks of the lovers fleeing into the trees.

III. 1922

The old woman is on her side on the sofa: the vase
Beside her is a fountain of red straw.
The old woman
Has been dead for some time now.

She drank her tea and stretched out on the sofa.
She looked out the open window
Across the street to where under the trees
The local orchestra was beginning something small
By Debussy. She watched a boy
Lift his tuba off the grass.
And with his first clear note she began to chill;
Her eyes never closed. She was just there
In her purple dress on the sofa. And
Through the open window all that night the boy
With the tuba was watched as if by an animal
Or monarch. You know how passengers

On a train prepare themselves
For a tunnel: they are watching the fir trees
That darken the hillsides while, separate and shy,
They begin to enter a mountain, they straighten
Under the white ropes and cool purple curtains:
There's a fat woman
Over there who neglects her lap dog and looks
As if she was stabbed in the neck, the banker
Beside you was maybe kicked by a horse in the head,
And even the child across from you

Stops sucking on her mother's breast and looks up
Having swallowed perhaps a coin or hatpin.

The victims of composition as dead passengers
On a train each secretly positioned
For a dark passage through rock where the ochre deer
Stand frozen, where everyone stops talking

To watch like the old woman on the sofa
Staring past her open window for a week, wanting
Very much to be discovered, she looks almost alive
Like the elephant gone perfectly still
In the mountain pass after hearing a train rush
By below him; he sniffs the air
And glances down into a forest where like him
Everything alive had stopped moving for a moment.
The train went by. The local orchestra sits
In its folding chairs and sips away at sherry,
All of them that is
But the boy with a tuba who looks
Across the street to an open window and further even

Into the dark house
Where nothing has moved for hours, where
You'll hear a voice that's not enough,
That speaks to us under the trees
Just before the white baton flies up:

What it says might be read aloud to children:
Tell me about the woman of many turns
Who had her tables cleaned with sponges
Who walked the beach like a motionless
Moving elephant
And who talked to the hyacinth, gull, and ant.
Tell me about the woman of many turns.

And tell me you can't . . .

Only if it had been a rainy morning
There wouldn't have been
The freshly cut flowers in the hall,
Or in the garden in the sun
The small toad wouldn't have thought her straw hat
Was a second sun that had cooled
Like everything else around her.
Only if it had rained along the coast
All that morning outside her open window.
If she wasn't in the garden in the morning
She would have been alive to see
The silver tuba like a snail
Returned to the grass after the concert.

The butterfly buttons its shirt twice
In the afternoon. After working
All morning in the garden she walked
Down to the ocean and looked across to France

Where the ochre deer have stood motionless
On the cave walls for centuries.
To the hyacinth she speaks French. She doesn't
Speak to us at all. This collector of black tea:
Souchong and Orange Pekoe brewed with the seeds
Of the St. Ignatius' bean, swallowed hurriedly
In the shade of a little country parlor. *She doesn't*

Speak to us at all.

Does the barbarian cutting the throat
Of a speckled doe in China ever enjoy his solitude?
Perhaps, he's always been alone
Like the corpse dressed in purple on the sofa.
They were both strong.
They have both eaten venison.
Their venison is historical and ochre.

How do we remember them? Let me
Tell you about this woman
Who's resting on the sofa
Like a fawn fading into leaves and rocks.
She's positioned for entering

A tunnel, and, yet, for her it was simply
An open window through which a boy
Reaches out for his tuba smiling

Like the Hun
Who's charging through the Empress Dowager's
Gardens, leaning down
From his horse he grabs a virgin by the hair
And lifts her off the grass

And having seen enough, this ordinary old woman
Saw an end to her suffering. *And, then,*

A white baton flew up!

JACOB BOEHME'S TRIPTYCH OF WINTER HOURS: 1620

There is fog in a meadow where bluebirds
Are wheeling and turning in the cold space:
There are young plane trees in snow looking
Like bell ropes that come out of low ceilings
From nowhere:
A thing can be desired only if it has
An opposite to resist it.
There could not be light without darkness.
There could not be good without evil.
There could not be a water crust in the well
Or a white light high up in the oak groves.
One warm summer night I
Left a pail of milk
Out on a windowsill to cool, and

I sat down at my table with friends
And put a lighted candle
On the blue, plated back of a wood louse
And announced that this plough horse of an insect
Would soon cross over all the way to the opposite
Edge of the table, but, you would say, what if the louse
Having reached the other edge had flown off
And out of the open window with Boehme's candle!
Would there have been, then, two morning stars
For your children?
Late that night with the light of
This candlestick I finished
The sentence I had begun nearly a year ago.
I wrote: and the ale is warm, as

The wings of this almost colorless insect are beating
With double vision, everywhere at once, the wings
Have become a waterwheel barely

Turning in a frozen stream beside a mill;
The illusion of the wings, now, is solid
Like a millstone *itself*:
A starling screams out in the purple brambles,
And can the beginning go to the end without
Beginning again, not like my wood louse dragged
Back again and again for my friends:
How he beat his wings, but then
The hot wax flooding down on him
Caught him in its cold form and just
Once more he painfully lifted his wings, and let

Them fall as an angel, petals of an oxeye daisy,
Or as two walls of a barn breaking in with heavy snow.

I I I

THE CITY OF
THE OLESHA
FRUIT

THE CITY OF THE OLESHA FRUIT

The spider vanished at the boy's mere
Desire to touch it with his hand.
                                    —*Yuri Olesha*

Outside the window past the two hills there is the city
Where the color-blind are waking to blue pears;
Also, there are the blue treetops waving
To the schoolgirls who step harshly along
In winter dresses: out of the mouths of these girls
Come the cones, their breath,
A mist like the silver ear trumpets
Of deaf children tipped toward whatever it is
They are almost hearing.

An old man without legs, not yet in a chair, has
Invented the city outside the window.
And everywhere now it is morning! He hears

His wife climbing the stairs.
What, he thinks . . . what to do?
The strong line of her back
Is like a spoon.
He says, "Good morning and how are you?"
She says, "Rumen,
I told you the hen should have been put
Up with straw in the attic. Last night the fox
Ate all but the dark spurs under her chin
And a few feathers."

His wife gathers him up in her arms, walks to the far
Corner of the room, and lowers him into a straight chair
Beside a table. Only last year he would sit
And stare at the shoes he could wear, without socks

And with the laces loose.
A tub is filling in another room.

He thinks, poor Widow is inside the stomach
Of a fox. My wife's idea was not a good one:
Where would Widow have found the scratch
And gravel for her shells while up in the attic?
And what about
The rooster! What about the poor rooster
On his railing by the barn; inconsolable, crowing?
Rumen remembers a Russian story about a copper rooster
With a green fern for a tail.
Rumen's favorite writer is the great Russian
Yuri Olesha. Rumen thinks, "Yes, Yuri, my companion,
There is cruelty in the format of a kiss!
And the blue skins of pears
In a heap on a dish leave a memory

Of myself as a boy running along the flume water
Down past the village ditch.
But, Yuri, in my city all the streets are,
Just this moment, being swept: old women
In jade dresses sweeping, sweeping.
And soon it will rain for them and then
I'll return their sun, a noon sun
To take away the wet before the children
Rush out under the bells for an hour's recess.

Oh, Yuri, beyond the grin of a smelly
Old fox, that's where Widow is, our best hen!
Yuri, my legs, I think, are buried in the orchard
Beside the stable where the hospital horses
Of my city wait, poised for an emergency.
These horses are constant; how they race
Down the cobbled streets for me. They've never
Trampled the children!"

"Rumen," his wife called, "do you want a haircut
This morning?" She steps into the room.

154

He smiles at her. She is buttoning her blouse.
And she smiles back to him. Rumen would say

To Yuri that sometimes her yellow hair
Got into the corners of his mouth.
"And, Yuri, that was when I most missed my youth."
Then Rumen would again fall silent.
He was off opening a raincloud over his city.
It was winter when he woke, but now I'm sure it's
Not. There are a few dark flowers?
Rumen feels that it is best for the children
If they walk to school in the clear winter air, but
Once he gets around to raining on his trees,
Streets and houses, well, then he changes everything
To late July and August.
But the evenings in his city are always
Placed in autumn: there is the smell
Of woodsmoke, so pleasant,
And leaves burning. Flocks of bluebirds would be
Flying south.

And so there is the obscurity of many lives,
Not yours, Olesha, but mine and my wife's,
Two characters
Who are, perhaps, in a shade
Just now sipping an iced summer tea
With its twigs and leaves floating around inside:

We are giggling, I think, about how shy
We were as lovers that first winter night
When I kissed her in the dark barn
Right in her open eye. I tried again
And missed again. To accidently kiss a young girl

In her open eye is, I think,
The beginning of experience. *Yuri*,
I did find her mouth that night!

But then the following winter, a week before
Our wedding, I missed again, this time
I kissed a small bare breast.
That wasn't an accident—

She reached out to touch my hand
And found my thigh!
The shyness of lovers, as softly, at night,
They miss and miss while following an old map, yes,
The format of a kiss.
In the city of the Olesha fruit

A citizen never dies, he just wakes
One morning without his legs, and then he is given
A city of his very own making:

In this way his existence narrows
While expanding like a diary, or
Like this landscape with two hills
Seen through my window early
Each and every winter morning! But, Yuri,
Outside this window—yes, I know,

What's there is there, and all of it
Indelible as our memory of blue pears, washed
And being eaten in the sunlight of a city
That is being constructed all of the time,
Its new gold domes and towers,
Just beyond two hills in the winter air, and
Somewhere inside the mind.

THE SEAGULL

CHEKHOV, AT YALTA

A winter evening at the cottage by the bay,
And I sat in the black and gold of the dead garden
Wrapped in blankets, eating my sister's suet pudding.
The fountain was wrapped in dirty straw and

Just below my property in the old Tartar cemetery
There is a small funeral in progress: the widow
Is wearing a purple shawl, the children are bare around
The shoulders and the girls are wearing orange petals

At their throats. The ashen white beards of the men
Are like immaculate vests from this distance.
There is nothing more intolerable than suet pudding,
Unless it is the visitors. The drunken visitors laughing

In my kitchen, eating my duck and venison, while I hide
From them here in the dark garden.
The daughter of one of these gentlemen is pretty.
I saw her through the window drinking

Champagne from a clay mug—under her thin blouse
I saw the blue points of her breasts that turn,
In opposition, both out and up like the azure slippers
Of the priest who is now singing in the cemetery below my house.

Once the family has gone off with its torches I'll
Climb down to the fresh grave and drop some coins
For flowers, even wooden teeth for the widow so she can

Attract a new husband? The black, turned soil
Of our garden reminds me
Of the common grave given to the children
Of the Godunov Orphanage after that horrible fire:

/ 5 7

A charred horse was thrown in with them,
Bags of lime and what I understood to be a large ham
That the authorities, nevertheless, declared
The torso of a male child of nine or ten. The Czar,

In their memory, placed a tiny trout pond over them
And this inscription: A *blue blanket for my little ones*.
My wife goes nearly naked to parties in Moscow.
My sister here, at Yalta, goes sea bathing with a rope

Around her that runs back to the beach where it is
Attached to a donkey who is commanded by a servant
With a long switch.
The sea tows her out and then the donkey is whipped

Sorrowfully until he has dragged her back to them.
I named the donkey, Moon, after the mystery of his service
To my sister. This winter
He has been an excellent friend.

I read to this poor beast from *Three Sisters*. He is a better
Critic and audience than I could find in the cities.
I have won an Award that will save me from arrest anywhere
Inside Russia. I am going to refuse it! And then travel

To Nice or Paris.
My tuberculosis is worse. Tolstoy reads my stories
To his family after supper. And reads them badly, I suppose!
I did walk that evening all the way down to the cemetery

Only to discover that my pockets were empty.
I screamed up to the house for coins, for plenty
Of coins! The visitors, laughing and singing, ran down
To me without coats and with a lantern swinging—

My sister trailed behind them
On her donkey. Her square black hat

Bobbing like a steamer way out in the bay.
And when they reached me—

I said, "Sister, pack the trunks! You hurt me!
I will write that we have departed for France, for Italy."

A WIDOW SPEAKS TO THE AURORAS OF
A DECEMBER NIGHT

My yard with its pines is almost spherical in winter.

The green awning outside the window is torn
By heavy snow. I sit in the cane chair.
Beside me, within reach, the gramophone grinds out
A little Debussy: the horn
Of the gramophone is plugged with a sock.

An artery stands out at my ankle
And these crossings
Of blood do blossom secretly in the leg, climbing
Up to the heart or lungs. There's the
Familiar light coming on in the distance in the dark city:

It has been a spark within a house above my pines
Before sunrise each winter for these
Past three years of just tea and the *Times*.
I often remember
An especially dry gin from the barroom
At the Ritz Tower. The watercolor my husband purchased
In Caracas remains in the corner
Bound in twine, and dark caramel papers; it has a
Big postage stamp depicting a native girl
Holding up a blue turtle.

The familiar light above the pines goes out. A man
Has dipped both of his hands into a stream of cold water.
He has washed his teeth and hair. Clean-shaven,
He greets his wife in the kitchen. She has fried
Some trout with bacon. Outside my window the sapphire light
Of the northeast-Packet plane lifts up out of Hartford,

Its soft, watery light dips and then
Leans into a sunrise:

There is snow, pines, and two sheep who have wandered
From a neighbor's farm beyond the reservoir—
Just this winter scene, and two wide sheep that
Are the blue-white of a chunk of fat

Falling off the dangerous, true edge of daylight.

AFTER THREE PHOTOGRAPHS OF
BRASSAÏ

A whore moves a basin of green antiseptic water
Away from the towels to a clean white shelf.
A Russian sailor rests against the wall smelling
Of tobacco.

The tall narrow mirror has little dark flecks
Within it like the black sinks of a smoky, surgical theater
Seen from the balconies: the whore
From *above* is now below us, in the future, on a table where

Two students in white gowns are struggling to open her:
The ribs cracking back, the pink gill-like trench
Follows the thin hairline down the center
Of her stomach to where the knife shallows on pelvic bone.

A student beside us vomits and his breakfast of warm milk
Falls slowly to the floor passing tier after tier
Of first-year students. The autopsy is over.
The charwoman in a yellow bonnet is mopping up.

Now the same dead girl is, again, moving the green water
Away from the soiled towels. A banker
Smelling of jasmine is dressing himself. The whore straightens
Her shoulders, this girl who is always bent

Over herself. Her fingers which she chews are hurt
By an acid douche. She straightens her shoulders
As she stares into a black speck in the mirror so as
To forget. She begins singing, also, to forget;

The banker stepping into his taxi is trying to remember
If there was a mole on her neck, if this one's name

Was Claudette? And he is stepping into the taxi, he is
Drunk and falling into the blackness of it: his shoe flies

Up into the night as high as the colored numerals and lights.
The door slams shut. The charwoman has finished mopping up,
She turns out the lights. You are now alone in the upper-
Most balcony looking down for a floor through the darkness.

You drop a pencil waiting to hear it strike the boards . . .
It falls stiff like a drunk, like a drunk falling onto a whore.

THE GANGES

I'm sorry but we can't go to the immersions tonight
For the poor will not get down from the wheel, and
The musicians and the lorry won't budge
Without the money. We don't have it. But, we could

Walk to the cremations. It will be dark with a mist
Where the stairs jump into the water. These are
The funeral ghats. The corpses are brought in drapes
And that one will be dipped in the river and then
She will be anointed with clarified butter. To the
Left of us four men waist deep in the river sift
Through mud and ashes for gold rings.
With a straw torch
The dead mother's son starts the fire;
With a bone cudgel
He smashes her skull to release the images shared
By her with these

Postcards I am now passing to you:
Of the family pond entirely filled with limes,
White pigs rooting in coconut husks, and her six
Children watering their charges, the black lulled elephants.

THE INFANT

> *There are possibilities for me, but under*
> *What stone, Father, do they lie?*
> —*Kafka*

Franz, under what stone. *You ask me under what stone?*
Knowing you, I would say—under *your* gravestone, in Prague.

You say that you can't write and yet at night you scribble
Until the light. You use paper like the successful bureaucrat

That you are. Vice Secretary of the Workers' Accident
Institute. And yet you insist that there is nothing

In this world you can do. You hate the grandchildren,
Their noises frighten you.

You write poor Felice and say that now you are in love
With another. It was a perfect setting for a romance,

The sanitorium in Riva! After troubling Felice with a rival,
And in the very same letter, you suddenly tell her

That you are on your knees, and will *she* be your wife?
You hurt her with silence. You hurt her when you write.

Martin Buber bores you.
Oklahoma bores you. Moses bores you.

Dead flowers on your desk excite you.
Rain excites you. And your sister's lacerated leg is all you'll

Hear of at the breakfast table!
Grete Bloch insists that we should grant your wish to live

In the woods with ghosts. Go then, will you? I'll throw the
Latch back on the door myself for you. I'll carry you

/ 6 5

To the woods. You love to lie on your mother's sofa
With a headache. When your sister bakes, you wait for her

Shout, and then you run down to us in glee to see a burn
Wrapped in stinging leaves.

Under stones, indeed; with the snakes, worms, and darning-fleas.
Yes, even for you there are possibilities.

Your disease is your desire
Not to be.

In the mousy darkness only the thought of cows
Keeps you from madness.

Your mother wishes you would help us with the coal bill.
I laughed. The truck driver laughed.

I look back to ask what I did wrong. What I hear
Is myself with you in my arms. When you were a baby

In your long gray gowns I sang to you the best songs.
I loved the one about the three-legged mule. And the

One where a giant sat on a toadstool.
You love the cat.

You watch it at its milk and then
Follow it to its box of sand. She arches her back.

And you make notes. You write that, at that moment, you have
No worries. What that vicious cat leaves in its box

You place in your novels—the undigested bones and tails
Of mice.

You, at your job, are so cold to the husky laborer who
Has a broken arm. But let the debtor, pensioner, whore

Come sobbing to you and you in tears respond, "Oh, isn't
It awful what happens to the weak and wronged."

You say that you can't deplore your selfishness, your
Silence, hypochondria, and tears, for they're the reflection

Of a higher consciousness that is impossible to understand.
To fear! *Franz,*

Don't lie. It's not under your gravestone that the possibilities
Lie, but here under mine. *And I survived you!*

Your mother and I today visited
Your grave at Strasniče. There was a black little acre

Beyond your grave off in the distance. Probably a potato field?
I made these words!

I'm not ashamed. *I will go off to eat*
A *large sandwich. Then, I will wash my feet.*

THE DUN COW AND THE HAG

Beside the river Volga near the village of Anskijovka
On a bright summer day

An old woman sat sewing
By the riverbank. If asked she would say

She was lowering the hem of a black dress.
All the while she sewed

A cow stood beside her. They were ignored
As the day passed; by evening, a merchant

From Novgorod arrived with his family
At the riverbank carrying baskets.

And his eldest daughter down beyond a clump
Of white birches undressed and stepped

Into the river, the girl's breasts
Are large and moved separately like twins

Handed from one serf to the next
Down to a river for baptism. The merchant,

His wife, and their son are seated
In the grass eating chunks of pink fish

That they dip in scented butter. The fish
Spoiled as it rode in the sun on the top

Of their carriage. These three have been poisoned
And can be seen kneeling in the grass.

The daughter who was bathing in the river
Is, now, crying for anyone to help her: the hag

Leaves her cow to walk down to the floundering girl:
Just her arms above the water

Working like scissors.
She cut the thread for the old woman.

It was summertime on the river Volga, and the old woman
Told the cow

That this could happen to anyone and that
It *had* happened once to them; and

It was summertime on the river Volga,
The black water

Ran off her dress like a lowered hem.

ELEGY TO THE SIOUX

The vase was made of clay
With spines of straw
For strength. The sun-baked vase
Soaked in a deep blue dye for days. The events in this wilderness,
Portrayed in the round of the vase,

Depend on shades of indigo against
The masked areas of the clay, a flat pearl color
To detail the big sky and snow . . .

This Montana field in winter is not sorrowful:
A bugle skips through notes:

We view it all somehow from the center of the field
And there are scattered groups of cavalry. Some of these
Men were seasoned by civil war. Their caps are blue.
Their canteens are frozen. The horses shake their heads
Bothered by the beads of ice, the needles of ice
Forming at both sides of their great anvil heads.

The long, blue cloaks of the officers fall over the haunches
Of the horses. The ammunition wagons
Beside the woods are blurred by the snowy weather . . .

Beyond the wagons, further even, into the woods
There is a sloping stream bed. This is
The dark side of the vase, which is often misunderstood.
From here through the bare trees there's
A strange sight to be seen at the very middle of the field:

A valet is holding a bowl of cherries—archetype and rubric,
A general with white hair eats the fruit while introducing its color,
Which will flow through the woods in early December.
An Indian woman came under dark clouds to give birth, unattended

In the deep wash inside the woods. She knew the weather

Could turn and staked the tips of two rooted spruce trees
To the earth to make a roof.
The deerskin of her robe is in her mouth. Her legs spread,
Her feet are tied up in the roof of darkening spruce. *No stars
Show through!* But on the vase that belonged to a President
There are countless stars above the soldier's campfires . . .

With rawhide her feet are tied high in the spruce
And her right hand is left loose as if she were about
To ride a wild stallion
                              to its conclusion in a box canyon.

President Grant drinks bourbon from his boot. The Sioux
Cough in their blankets . . .

It snowed an hour more, and then the moon appeared.
The unborn infant,
Almost out on the forest floor, buckled and lodged. It died.
Its mother died. Just before she closed her eyes
She rubbed snow up and down the inside of her bare thighs.

In the near field an idle, stylish horse raised one leg
To make a perfect right angle. Just then a ghost of snow formed
Over the tents of the soldiers,

It blows past the stylish, gray horse,
Unstopped it moves through woods, up the stream bed
And passes into the crude spruce shelter, into the raw open
Woman, her legs raised into sky—
Naked house of snow and ice! This gust of wind

Spent the night within the woman. At sunrise, it left her mouth
Tearing out trees, keeping the owls from sleep; it was angry now
And into the field it spilled, into the bivouac of pony soldiers

Who turned to the south, who turned back to the woods, who became

Still. Blue all over! If there is snow
Still unspooling in the mountains
Then there is time yet for the President to get his Indian vase
And to fill it with bourbon from his boot and to put flowers into it:
The flowers die in a window that looks out on a cherry tree
Which heavy with fruit drops a branch:
                              torn to its very heartwood
By the red clusters of fruit, the branch fell
Like her leg and foot
Out of the big sky into Montana . . .

A GRANDFATHER'S LAST LETTER

Elise, I have your valentine with the red shoes, I have
Waited too many weeks to write—wanting to describe
The excitement on the back lawn for you:
                              the forsythia

Is now a bright yellow, and with the ribbons you draped
Inside it, trembles in a breeze,
All yellows and blues, like that pilot light this winter
Worried by just a little breath that came out of you.

On the dark side of the barn there's the usual railing
Of snow.
The tawny owl, nightingales, and moles
Have returned to the lawn again.

I have closed your grandmother's front rooms.

I know you miss her too. Her crocus bed showed its first
Green nose this morning. For breakfast I had
A duck's egg and muffins.

Your father thinks I shouldn't be alone?
Tell him I have planted a row of volunteer radishes.
I have replaced the north window . . .

So you have read your first book. Sewed a dress for
The doll. The very young and old are best at finding
Little things to do. The world is jealous of us, you know?

The moles are busy too. Much more mature this year,
The boar with the black velvet coat made a twelve
Foot long gallery under the linden where the mockingbirds
Are nesting.

73

The moles took some of my rags to add to
Their nursery of grass, leaves, and roots.
The cream-colored sow is yet to make her appearance!
They have seven mounds. Each with three bolt doors
Or holes.
The pine martens are down from the woods, I see them
In the moonlight waiting for a kill.

Molehills can weaken a field so that a train
Passing through it sinks suddenly, the sleepers
In their berths sinking too!

I wonder what it's like in their underground rooms:
Their whiskers telegraphing the movements
Of earthworms. They don't require water when on
A steady diet of nightcrawlers. Worms are almost
Entirely made of water.

Last night there was quite an incident. The sun was going
Down and the silly boar was tunneling toward
The linden and he went shallow, the owl dropped down
Setting its claws into the lawn, actually taking hold
Of the blind mole, at that moment the mockingbird,
Thinking her nest threatened, fell on the owl putting
Her tiny talons into his shoulders. Well,

There they were, Elise, the owl on top of the invisible
Mole, the mockingbird on top of the owl. The mole
Moved backwards a foot,
The birds were helpless and moved with him.
They formed quite a totem. The two birds looked so serious
In their predicament. A wind brushed the wash on the line.
And our three friends broke each for its respective zone.

Tomorrow the vines on the house are coming down. I want
The warmth of the sun on that wall. I'm sending

You a package with some of your grandmother's old clay
Dolls, silverware, and doilies.

Tell your father he is not coming in June to kill
The moles! Tell him to go fishing instead, or to take
Your mother to Florida.

You said you worry that someday I'll be dead also! Well,
Elise, of course, I will. I'll be hiding then from your world
Like our moles. They move through their tunnels
With a swimming motion. They don't know where they're going—

But they go.

There's more to this life than we know. If ever
You're sleeping in a train on the northern prairies
And everything sinks a little
But keeps on going, then, you've visited me in another world—

Where I am going.

ELEGY TO THE PULLEY OF SUPERIOR OBLIQUE

Weston's photograph of a border bridge

The three girls in a donkey cart are
Ascending the tiled adobe bridge, its little arc
Over the dry wash under a noonday sun. Below them
A wizened farmer with a bag of grain sleeps in the shadows
Of the bridge while sitting on the dry river
Bottom which looks like a long black skid mark
Vanishing off the side of a cliff on the highway beyond
The purple mountains.

There are miserable people, standing for the duration
In a halated light, whom I would never describe

For it would be a lie. To write, for example, that
Two house flies are like two fiddles drying
In a mahogany vise beside
The blue chisels and almond pastes, that all over the shop
Fans are blowing across huge blocks of ice—
That would be a lie! There's blood on an apron and
The green checkered bills in the cigar box. And
The carpenter's wife is a Jew. This is Warsaw ten years
Before my birth. The sweltering ghetto! Months later,
The sweltering snow!

So I must tell you that the sisters in the cart are
Unhappy and not beautiful. They have suffered scabs and
Diarrhea. They have boiled water out in their yard,
Beside the deep, fragrant cilia plants, and had been too weak
To drag the scalded water a foot or two beyond the fire.
They have all fainted, once or twice,
While squatting in the trench out behind their barn.
This influenza killed their mother. And aunt.

And, now, they have crossed the bridge and the donkey
Looks under his belly; slumps to one side, and falls
Dead.
The younger sister begins to sob.
The oldest jumps from the cart and runs down a pebble slope
To the sleeping farmer.
The farmer wakes, frightened, not for a moment looking
Away from the girl's chest that is running with sores.
He says, "A man is taking our picture from above!"
The toothless farmer then waves to Weston, and
The girl slumps onto the brown river bed with her arms
Around herself.
There are dogs sniffing near the donkey.
There are two flies. And

What does this girl have to do with
Our lives? That excellent man, *Rosen*, knows:

Open your eyes: there's sky, mountains; the moment
Of death is instant, contrived.

THE OLD ASYLUM OF THE NARRAGANSETTS

A dark Pilgrim couple in white bibs walks along a barricade of logs

To the blockhouse within which
Two cloaked figures, in candlelight, stand and study
Mistress Sheffield's goose, nailed to the narrow door
By clergy. John Sheffield's children, at dusk,
Struggle through the snow carrying two baskets of honey calabash.

There's a fire beside the old saltboxes of the Waterfront,
A wood smoke with the nauseous, weighted odor
Of night-flowering phlox. Below the piers, the Atlantic

Sleeps in the sheltered harbor.

The Magistrate's dogs are running a deer out across
The saltmarsh. On Burial Hill fresh graves are ignited
With dropped bundles of Poinsettia, and here a Pilgrim
Nests like a page of testament, bound
By abundant scripture. The small Plymouth choir
In red shawls scatters voices along
The street, down around the corner
To the Governor's gabled house where in the upper window
Candles are moving in a sickroom—

The Governor's niece has contracted cholera!

The pious physician sits in a chair and eats steadily from
A plate of Mistress Blaisdale's caramel divinity, peppermints,
And marzipan. At morning, he'll find the sick girl
Sitting under her cap,
Eyes open—with fever broken; hours later from the balcony,
The Governor with arms extended above the wilderness
Sings his proclamation of joy, and,

This early November morning, the treetops on the hill
Are inky with intervals of opalescent sky
That's fired by the sunrise. The shadows along the Waterfront
Will expel an Indian in a dugout,
A still warm doe roped around his neck and shoulders;

The lowing cows wear bells of brass and antimony,

Their silhouettes across the pasture of the Common
Are like small bobbing ships, processional
And violet in the wintry canals
Of Holland . . . the witch, Mistress Sheffield,
Is in her coffin, the creamy marl

Of her hands at her neck,
The dagger drinking there: a dragonfly beaded with amethyst,
Its wings beating invisibly
Like the cold puritan heart exalted above its wilderness.

THOMAS HARDY

The first morning after anyone's death, is it important
To know that fields are wet, that the governess is
Naked but with a scarf still covering her head, that
She's sitting on a gardener who's wearing
Just a blue shirt, or that he's sitting on a chair in the kitchen.
They look like they are rowing while instead outside in the mist
Two boats are passing on the river, the gardener's mouth
Is opening:

A white, screaming bird lifts off the river into the trees,
Flies a short distance, and is joined
By a second bird, but then as if to destroy everything
The two white birds are met by a third. *The night
Always fails.* The cows are now standing in the barns.
You can hear the milk as it drills into wooden pails.

YOU

The sunlight passes through the window into the room
Where you are sewing a button to your blouse: outside
Water in the fountain rises
Toward a cloud. This plume of water is lighter
Now, for white shares of itself are falling back
Toward the ground.
This water does succeed, like us,
In nearing a perfect exhaustion,
Which is its origin. The water

Succeeds in leaving the ground but
It fails at its desire to reach a cloud. It pauses,
Falling back into its blue trough; of course,
Another climb is inevitable, and this loud, falling
Water is a figure for love, not loss, and

Still heavy with its desire to be the cloud.

ELIZABETH'S WAR WITH THE
CHRISTMAS BEAR

The bears are kept by hundreds within fences, are fed cracked
Eggs; the weakest are
Slaughtered and fed to the others after being scented
With the blood of deer brought to the pastures by Elizabeth's
Men—the blood spills from deep pails with bottoms of slate.

The balding Queen had bear gardens in London and in the country.
The bear is baited: the nostrils
Are blown full with pepper, the Irish wolf dogs
Are starved, then, emptied, made crazy with fermented barley:

And the bear's hind leg is chained to a stake, the bear
Is blinded and whipped, kneeling in his own blood and slaver, he is
Almost instantly worried by the dogs. At the very moment that
Elizabeth took Essex's head, a giant brown bear
Stood in the gardens with dogs hanging from his fur . . .
He took away the sun, took
A wolfhound in his mouth, and tossed it into
The white lap of Elizabeth I—arrows and staves rained

On his chest, and standing, he, then, stood even taller, seeing
Into the Queen's private boxes—he grinned
Into her battered eggshell face.
Another volley of arrows and poles, and opening his mouth
He showered
Blood all over Elizabeth and her Privy Council.

The next evening, a cool evening, the Queen demanded
13 bears and the justice of 113 dogs: She slept

All that Sunday night and much of the next morning.
Some said she was guilty of *this* and *that*.
The Protestant Queen gave the defeated bear

A grave in a Catholic cemetery. The marker said:
Peter, a Solstice Bear, a gift of the Tsarevitch to Elizabeth.

After a long winter she had the grave opened. The bear's skeleton
Was cleared with lye, she placed it at her bedside,
Put a candle inside behind the sockets of the eyes, and, then
She spoke to it:

You were a Christmas bear—behind your eyes
I see the walls of a snow cave where you are a cub still smelling
Of your mother's blood which has dried in your hair; you have
Troubled a Queen who was afraid
When seated in *shade* which, standing,
You had created! A Queen who often wakes with a dream
Of you at night—
Now, you'll stand by my bed in your long white bones; alone, you
Will frighten away at night all visions of bear, and all day
You will be in this cold room—your constant grin,
You'll stand in the long, white prodigy of your bones, and you are,

Every inch of you, a terrible vision, not bear, but virgin!

AUBADE OF THE SINGER AND
SABOTEUR, MARIE TRISTE

In the twenties, I would visit Dachau often with my brother.
There was then an artists' colony outside the Ingolstadt Woods
And these estates had a meadow filled
With the hazy blood-campion, sumac, and delicate yellow cinquefoil.
At the left of the meadow there was a fast stream and pond, and
Along the stream, six lodges and the oak Dachau Hall where
Meals were held and the evening concerts. In winter, the Hall was a
Hostel for hunters, and the violinists, who were the first
Of the colony to arrive in spring, would spend three days
Scouring the deer blood off the floors, tables, walls, and sinks.
They would rub myrtle leaves into the wood to get out the stink!

The railway from Munich to Ingolstadt would deposit us by
The gold water tower, and my brother, Charles, and I would cut
Across two fields to the pastures behind Dachau Hall. Once,
Crossing these fields, Charles, who had been drinking warm beer
Since morning, stopped, and crouching low in the white chicory
And lupine found a single, reddish touch-me-not which is rare
Here in the mountains. A young surgeon, Charles assumed his
Condescending tone, and began by saying, "Now, sister,

This flower has no perfume—what you smell is not your
Brother's breath either, but the yeast sheds of the brewery just over
That hill. This uncommon flower can grow to an enormous height
If planted in water. It is a succulent annual. Its private
Appointments are oval and its nodding blossom takes its weight
From pods with crimson threadlike supports." With his bony fingers

He began to force open the flower. I *blushed*. He said, "It is
A devoted, sexual flower; its tough, meatlike labia protrude
Until autumn and then shrivel; this adult flower

If disturbed explodes *into a small yellow rain like*
That fawn we watched urinating on the hawthorn just last August."

Charles was only two years older but could be a wicked fellow.
Once, on our first day at the colony, at midnight, he was
Discovered nude and bathing in the pond with a cellist. She was
The only cellist, and for that week, Charles was their only doctor.
So neither was banished. But neither was spoken to except
For rehearsals and in illness. There is a short bridge passage
In a Scriabin sonata that reminds me of the bursting touch-me-nots.
That reminds me, also, of Heisdt-Bridge *itself,* in Poland! We blew
It up in October. I had primed the packages of glycerin, kieselguhr,
Woodmeal, and chalk. We curbed the explosives with sulphur.
I sat in primrose and sorrel with the plunger box and at four o'clock
Up went the munitions shipment from Munich to Warsaw. Those thin
Crimson supports of the flower tossed up like the sunburned arms
Of the pianist Mark Meichnik, arriving at his favorite E-flat
Major chord; and I guess that whenever a train or warehouse went
Four-ways-to-market right before my eyes, I thought
Of that large moment of Schumann's. The morning
After Heidst-Bridge I was captured and Charles

Was shot.

I was at Dachau by the weekend. They have kept me in
A small cell. A young Lieutenant tortured me that first night.
Knowing I was a singer they asked me to perform
For the Commandant early the next week.
By then I was able to stand again, but my Nazi inquisitor
Had for an hour touched live wires to me while holding
Me in a shallow ice bath. I had been
Made into a tenor voice! The Commandant's wife dismissed me
After a few notes. As I was tortured I forced myself
To dwell on the adult life of the touch-me-not, that fawn in
Hawthorn, and my brother's drunken anatomy lesson that showed
No skill at all there in the silver meadow. I was probably

Stupid not to have fallen unconscious. When I was
Ordered out of the parlor by the Nazi bitch, I did, for the first

Time in two years, cry aloud. I think it was for my voice that
I cried so badly. The guards laughed, returning me to my cell.
My cell has a bench, a pail, and a wire brush. Every two days
Without warning the hose comes alive with water, moving through
The space like a snake. Sometimes it wakes me about the face and legs.
I have lost so much weight that I can sleep comfortably
On the pine bench. I watch shadows in the cell become,
At night, the masquerade dance in the woodcut by Hans Burgkmair:

Its bird shapes, that procession of *men* threading the dance,
And *Maximillian I* greeting them as they twist past the banquet tables.
My inquisitor, all night in the chamber, commanding me
To sing, to sing!

When they fire the ovens out beside the pastures it is like
A giant catching his breath. And then there is the silence
Of the trucks with their murmuring engines. My delusions:
A sound like my brother's cellist, at this early hour, opening
The morning with difficult arm exercises; he said that she would
Play for him naked and until he became jealous. Then I would
Say, "Oh, Charles!" He'd laugh.

My favorite pastime has become the imaginary destruction of flowers.
I hear their screams. They bleed onto the floor of my cell. I scrub
The wall where a *bürgermeister* opened the artery of a doe that
He had shot just outside the window.
Later, the *Bürgermeister's* favorite butcher making venison flanks
Into roasts, how he sawed at the large femur of the deer
Like the cellist waking with her instrument, their right arms
Are beautiful with white muscles;
The butcher and the cellist died, here, admiring the noxious
Blue crystals on the floors of the gas chamber: the way,

At first, they darken to indigo and like smoke
Climb over your ankles, reaching your waist—
You fall naked as into the field that is with a breeze turning
All its wildflowers, bladder-campion and myrtle, into
A melody of just three staves written for four voices:

Slaughter and music.
Two of the old miracles. They were not my choices.

I V

THE

EVERLASTINGS

COMES WINTER, THE SEA HUNTING

For my daughter

This was your very first wall, your crib against
The wall that was papered in a soft
Fawn color, the powdered wings of a moth
Slowing in the cobwebs of the window—

The moth, poor like us, died
In her paper dress on stilts. The spider
Is a monarch, fat in
Winter chambers, the articles of her
Wealth are also
The articles of the kill: a little narcotic with silk!

We had two rooms in a blue, collapsing roadhouse
At the very lip of a valley
With a deep river and woods. The house
Had been settling for a century.
Those dizzying, tin
Trapezoid rooms . . .
A house built on rock, a rock built on sand,

And while I slept, your mother, who was
Big with you, hammered from silver—

A knife! A spoon! You,
On a crescent of bone, sleep
A sleep of plums: moisture on the plum forms a window

And inside everything reclines tasting meat and wine
From mid-day
Until evening. *That winter came in terms of you . . .*

The wet pods on sticks, mimes playing
Dice in a blizzard! Out of fields of rice come women

From the North, dark pajamas full of explosives . . .
Your mother now is
Naked and dreaming in the corner,
Is the Elder Breughel's inverted, golden doe
On a green pole, being
Shouldered back to the winter village.

Inside a box by the stairs there's an egg
Halved by a hair,
A box filled with sleep and even the retired ferryman,
George Sharon, leaving
Us two bottles of milk in the morning,
Would not look into it!
The cedar balcony in the back took its weight

In ice, first, three large icicles, then five,
And finally a webbing, in between, of thin ice.
The balcony was sealed
In a wall of crystals. With your new spoon
I carved into this blue-green wall

Dürer's *Sky Map*
Of the Northern Hemisphere: the silver, ancestral
Figures of crab, spectacle bear,
And *Bootes* with his long pink muscles and spear:

On clear nights the opaque stars above Montpelier
Appeared through this sky chart.

Up in the corner, where
'the fish with spilled pitcher' should be,
There was instead
A bat, snow had
Brought the roof in on him and he was
Caught in ice, hanging by a claw in the eaves.

I called him
Pipistrelle, old and dead flittermouse, he was

A reach of bone and a square of fur like a squirrel
Nailed out on a red barn in October. Pipistrelle,
At the corners of his wings, had blackened stars. Valiant

Dürer's sky map
Was now different with these triangular ears—
The dead pipistrelle carries a sound picture
That is like our memory of the dark trees, or the spaces
Between the old ferryman's teeth.
The bat would use its wings
Like oars; rowing in the blackish cataracts
Of a winter porch: star room! Lamp room . . .

The winter comes,

A *sea hunting*, and your father after sleeping
Puts his fist into the star wall, making a hole;
The wind entered

Moving at the height of the unborn,
This wind erased the lights of hemispheres!
That night, a breaking of ice, and the next morning
The bag-of-waters begins seeping as your
Mother tries a flight of stairs—

An old woman puts a horn to her stomach, and
Listens for you,

You have formed from seawater:
A deep luminous eye, digits, a bridge for a nose—
Abstract, monstrous—you have two oars!
You can only hear the ferryman in the cove,
Walking with his ladder, he somehow hangs his lamp
On the tall pole.

In an earlier season,

You were conceived, touched by *two* sounds of water
In a gulf; you formed your pulse, little patch over nothing,

Drawn in and drawn out—this is the meaning as,
Sadly and much later, a feather
Or candle is put to our mouths!

There were
Agates on the windowsill and a vase of dry pussywillows;

The out-larged map-maker's instruments boiling
Before labor, the towels and basins,
A hatching
In the ruby rhomboidal rooms where

A spider on her lucent thread
Swings into sunlight, then leaves us climbing up
A silken helix to eaves and

Pigeon gloom, but

You have washed up in the surf, and look out over
A new light like water showing,
Another mother,

A first attempt for someone loved, as
Out of her dress dropped in a circle—this nude,
The steady spectre at your birth,
Steps near to kiss you, circle of goldsmith's blue;
The pipistrelles fan the air . . .
This world would deceive us

So live in it as two! This was the very first wall
                    that you had to have passed through . . .

DOUBLE SPHERE, CLOVEN SPHERE

The black clouds swell up around the setting sun
Making a distant elm conspicuous,
Its rosy domination like the claw

On a garden rake held up
Before the face and through which
The blinking leaf fires of late autumn play.

The blue sheafs
Of tree shadows fall across the doorway where
A man and a woman are speaking, looking at their feet,
In the yard full of leaves.

He repeats a simple sentence. The long sleeves
Of her gray sweater will swallow her hands
As she dances a little in place, cold and impatient!

But they are both in pain.

A wet December day has made their naked bodies linger
Like red berries in the memory.

It ends over white papers with a stranger
Who awards the man two chairs, who awards the woman
A sofa and mirror.

They begin to walk away, in opposite directions,
Kicking up leaves—tears down their faces . . .

This farewell was both simple and difficult.
The incalculable
Ditches in the field below their cold house
Are touched with mist; ice

Forms in the stubble. *These were our times*.

And the slumbering ruse of early winter
Points a long finger in the direction
Of our exile:
                    a passage that's all so clear
Taking us over the horizon into atmosphere.

THE FOX WHO WATCHED FOR THE
MIDNIGHT SUN

Across the snowy pastures of the estate
Open snares drift like paw prints under rain, everywhere
There is the conjured rabbit being dragged
Up into blowing snow: it struggles
Upside down by a leg, its belly
Is the slaked white of cottages along the North Sea.

Inside the parlor Ibsen writes of a summer garden, of a
Butterfly sunken inside the blossoming tulip.
He describes the snapdragon with its little sconce of dew.
He moves from the desk to a window. Remembers his studies
In medicine, picturing the sticky
Overlapping eyelids of drowned children. On the corner
Of the sofa wrapped in Empress-silks there's a box
Of fresh chocolates. He mimics the deceptively distant,
Chittering birdsong within the cat's throat.
How it attracts finches to her open window.
He turns toward the fire, now thinking of late sessions in Storting.
Ibsen had written earlier of an emotional girl
With sunburnt shoulders,

Her surprise when the heavy dipper came up
From the well with frogs' eggs bobbing in her water.
He smiles.

Crosses the room like the fox walking away
From the woodpile.
He picks up his lamp and takes it
To the soft chair beneath the window. Brandy is poured.
Weary, he closes his eyes and dreams
Of his mother at a loom, how she would dip, dressing
The warp with a handful of coarse wool.

Henrik reaches for tobacco—tomorrow, he'll write
Of summer once more, he'll begin with a fragrance . . .
Now, though, he wonders about the long
Devotion of his muscles to his bones, he's worried by
The wind which hurries the pages in this drafty room.
He looks out
Into the March storm for an illustration: under a tree
A large frozen hare swings at the end of a snare string.
The fox sits beneath it, his upturned head swinging with it,
The jaws are locked in concentration,

As if the dead hare were soon to awaken.

THE COMPOSER'S WINTER DREAM

Vivid and heavy, he strolls through dark brick kitchens
Within the great house of Esterhazy:
A deaf servant's candle
Is tipped toward bakers who are quarreling about
The green kindling! The wassail is
Being made by pouring beer and sherry from dusty bottles

Over thirty baked apples in a large bowl: into
The wassail, young girls empty their aprons of
Cinnamon, ground mace, and allspice berries. A cook adds
Egg whites and brandy. The giant, glass snifters
On a silver tray are taken from the kitchens by two maids.
The anxious pianist eats the edges of a fig

Stuffed with Devonshire cream. In the sinks the gall bladders
Of geese are soaking in cold salted water.
Walking in the storm, this evening, he passed
Children in rags, singing carols; they were roped together
In the drifting snow outside the palace gate.
He knew he would remember those boys' faces . . .

There's a procession into the kitchens: larger boys, each
With a heavy shoe of coal. The pianist sits and looks
Hard at a long black sausage. He will not eat

Before playing the new sonata. Beside him
The table sags with hams, kidney pies, and two shoulders
Of lamb. A *hand rings a bell in the parlour!*

No longer able to hide, he walks
Straight into the large room that blinds him with light.
He sits before the piano still thinking of hulled berries . . .
The simple sonata which

He is playing has little
To do with what he's feeling: something larger
Where a viola builds, in air, an infinite staircase.
An oboe joins the viola, they struggle
For a more florid harmony.
But the silent violins now emerge,

And like the big wind of a bird, smother everything
In a darkness from which only a single horn escapes—
That feels effaced by the composer's dream . . .
But he is not dreaming,
The composer is finishing two performances simultaneously!

He is back in the dark kitchens, sulking and counting
His few florins—they have paid him
With a snuffbox that was pressed
With two diamonds, in Holland!
This century discovers quinine.
And the sketchbooks of a mad, sad musician

Who threw a lantern at his landlord who was standing beside
A critic. *He screamed: here, take a snuffbox, I've filled*
It with the dander of dragons! He apologizes
The next morning, instructing the landlord to take
This *stuff* (Da Ist Der Wisch) to a publisher,
And sell it! *You'll have your velvet garters, Pig!*

The composer is deaf, loud, and feverish . . . he went
To the countryside in a wet sedan chair.
He said to himself: for the piper, seventy ducats! He'd curse
While running his fingers through his tousled hair, he made
The poor viola climb the stairs.
He desired loquats with small pears!

Ludwig, there are spring bears under the pepper trees!
The picnic by the stone house . . . the minnows
Could have been sunlight striking fissures
In the stream; Ludwig, where your feet are

In the cold stream
Everything is horizontal like the land and living.

The stream said, "In the beginning was the word
And without the word
Was not anything made that was made . . .
But let us believe in the word, Ludwig,
For it is like the sea grasses
Off which the giant snails eat, at twilight!" But then

The dream turns to autumn; the tinctures he
Swallows are doing nothing for him, and he shows
The physicians his spoon which has dissolved
In the mixtures the chemist has given him!
After the sonata was heard; the standing for applause
Over, he walked out where it was snowing.

It had been dark early that evening. It's here that the
Dream becomes shocking: he sees a doctor
In white sleeves
Who is sawing at the temporal bones of his ears. There is
A bag of dampened plaster for the death mask, and
Though he *is* dead, a pool of urine runs to the

Middle of the sickroom. A brass urinal is on the floor, it is
The shape of his ears rusting on gauze. The doctors

Drink stale wassail. They frown over the dead Beethoven. Outside,
The same March storm that swept through Vienna an hour before
Has turned in its tracks like the black, caged panther
On exhibit in the Esterhazys' candlelit ballroom. The storm crosses
Over Vienna once more: lightning strikes the Opera House, its eaves
And awning filled with hailstones,
Flames leaping to the adjacent stables! Someone had known,
As thunder dropped flower boxes off window sills,
Someone *must* have known
That, at this moment, the violins would emerge
In a struggle with the loud, combatant horns.

THE NIGHT BEFORE THANKSGIVING

A grove of deep sycamores drifts into the Hudson,
The blue lights on a sledge
Go white as it drags its iron nets
Slowly up the trench of the river:
Inside an old Studebaker, my father sits beside a meadow.
Next to him there's a hot thermos, and a little box
Of codeine tablets for the pain in his knee. He reaches
Over into the backseat for a red, plaid blanket; it has
White hair on it from a long-dead cat. The blanket

Goes over his lap—at that moment, a giant
Spectacle moth settles like a falling hazel leaf on the blanket:
The moth, powdered in lime and chalk, has a lurid green
Eye on each forewing: it has come to my father after
A long season of feeding
From the night-flowering sweet tobacco!
The spectacle moth has settled and died, and there is
The smell of burning gasoline. On the river, a horn blows
Twice from a lamp room that is followed by barges loaded
With coal; flames from a foundry climb over pine trees that
Are miles down the road . . .
Across the water there are lanterns
Over the lawns of a mansion where women

In long gowns are playing croquet without wickets. These women
Are drinking; they laugh and wave to
The lonely, bored man in the tugboat who pulls on the horn again.
My father waves to him; the moth closes
Its shattered ice-green eyes like a blackened coal miner
Stepping out of a mountain into winter daylight.

ODE TO THE SPECTRAL THIEF, ALPHA

> *The stream silent as if empty. Dusk in the*
> *mirrors. Doors shutting.*
> *Only one woman without a pitcher remains*
> *in the garden—*
> *Made of water, transparent in moonlight, a*
> *flower in her hair!*
> *—Yannis Ritsos*

The way grapes will cast a green rail,
With tendrils and flowers, out along
A broken fence, down the edge of a field:
Then, climbing over hawthorn and up
Into the low branches of an elm. The moon

Is also up in the branches of the elm along with
A raccoon who sits and fills himself
On the dark, dusty fruit—under the branch,
On which the raccoon is situated,
His deep brown feces splatter over
Queen Anne's Lace and the waving sedge
Of the pond . . .

An owl lifts out of the tufted, solitary orchard
And there are hot-silver zig-zags, lightning
Up in the fat black clouds; this quiet
Before an August storm is nothing at all
Compared to the calm after a snowfall . . .
But the long boxes of hay in the field
Will stand, they are dense coffins
In which small living things

Are caught, broken: mouse, grasshopper,
And the lame sparrow. The field looks down
To an old quarry and road, and across
To a dark beach on the Atlantic.

Stone from the quarry built a small
Custom's House out on the Point.
Its old form is in ruin, now! But bells are
Still heard out there just before dawn:
Their purpose must fade over the water . . .

The water knows the three formal elements
That should compose an ode: say it, *élan!*
There's turn and counter-turn . . .
And turn, again; not *stand!*
The epode has a talent for rattling a tambourine
Like pie tins strung across a garden
To frighten, at night, the subtle, foraging deer.

The epode knows about fear; but, shaking
In its bones, I've said it has a talent for
Playing the tambourine by ear.
The raccoon struggling out of his tree
Doesn't care about
The eye, bait, and teeth of a Windsor Trap;
The pie tins, touched by a wind moving
Over the spears of corn, do not

Confuse him.
He wanders off into the orchard and down
Into a fast stream where suddenly
A grinning hound stops him—
The coon rears up on his haunches like a bear,
Spits and screams: his claws tear
At the weeping eyes of the big dog: turned twice,

The hound bites into fur, meat, and *then*
Deep into the spilled milk of the spine. This is
When the stream seems empty, silent!
This is also where the story divides in my mind.
What can I tell you?

Only that in past centuries
There were fewer
Dimensions to any concept of time,
And there was a greater acceptance of mirrors, and rhyme.

THE PARALLAX MONOGRAPH FOR RODIN

I dreamt, last night, of your stone cabinet, *Porte de l'Enfer*,
Everything was there, except it had turned into
The doors of an elevator in an old hotel of potted ferns. I'm certain
That outside the hotel there was a beach with, here and there, a colorful
But faded umbrella! I said it wasn't changed, but that's not fair;
I hesitate to say this but *the contemplative*, with his head
Resting on his fist, was replaced, in the dream, by a clock
That somehow told the time of day and the location of the elevator!
The face of all this work seemed unchanged, still a clamoring
Of naked men and women, not religious but ordered
In their desperation.

My favorite figure remains: the woman on the far right just below
The strong backside of a man who's assisted in his climb: his left foot
Lifts from her extended left hand and arm—her hair cannot be
Described, omitted as if swept aside by a severe comb,
Her breast is young but not exactly firm.
I don't really know if she assists
The man above her or if this was just an opportunity he seized;
After all, his right foot rests on a head that has no body.
I sense their community as being *of oblivion*. Outside
This hotel elevator the unbaptized infants wait, unwashed and
Smoking green cigars, they are delayed, in limbo . . .

The dream has worked a parody of your dark, portal scene,
Deus ex machina, and your intense belief in a teeming life

That struggles for relief out of a slab of rock in which
You saw it all from the very beginning: helmets, wings, thighs,
Breasts, hands, ankles, mouths, and even the small cherub peeing
In the cracked mirror. The mirror is the mouth of an obese banker
From Reims. Everything you made
Was placed in an enclosing but not final space. Only the most

Brilliant comedian possesses your gestures in their correct
Abstract mathematical sequence. I think by now

We must be alone!
My bored reader having left us both for a fresh lettuce sandwich—
Sometimes abstraction suits me like throwing rocks
In a building with a simple clerestory of stained glass. *We should
Discuss light.* It has suggestive, serial properties like a girl's loud
Orgasm in a drifting rowboat over a peaceful river, at night.
Let's pretend the lovers in the rowboat have drifted for nearly
A kilometer, and now, at the moment that she announces
Her arrival at this thunderstruck height, her lover discovers
They have floated up to a dock filled with aristocrats
At a party with lap dogs, wine, and hanging lanterns . . .

The girl is sitting on the boy, the rowboat rocks gently.
The boy's nakedness is lost, made modest, by his partner's
Large thighs and buttocks, she
Is indifferent to the strangers on the dock; she goes on
Screaming the boy's name, and the rowboat drifts past,
Back into the shadows of the trees that contain the river.
Wonderful! The aristocrats are bent in stitches of laughter.

I was talking about your comical gestures, and an obscure thought
That discouraged my reader, who left for a sandwich. To punish
Him I have invented this charming vignette of pleasure
Which he's missed!
He thinks little of your materials: there's strings, wires, planes, and
Cubes. The vertical sequences of nudes. You appraised a nude
Like a sturdy chair or stool.

The way you place Balzac's head in that massive unfinished neck,
His face is like a smashed gem in matrix.
The apprehension of chiaroscuro, as in the lines of a daffodil, is
Not your style. The princess, David, of Donatello is not your style!
Anything free-standing like a glutton in an English garden *is*
Your style.

The infants, unwashed, still smoking cigars, in front of your elevator,
Have begun a card game; they curse and spit but are not offensive.

Rodin, I've put off saying this, but your male secretary is sad
And disheartened . . .
He writes with power about the corpse on the kitchen table.
In triplicate, he's sent an application, listing grievances, to the stars!
He operates your old elevator in that dream hotel.
He's left everyone in the lurch; ground level. What's he doing now
That instructs the summer guests to undress and climb the walls?
Tortured and naked, they seem to have little patience with him.
His name? The real key is silver on a chain streaming from his pocket.

Your secretary is on the roof of the hotel having a smoke
While looking out over the ocean. He has been joined by two waiters.
They gaze out over the water, remembering the quiet
Days of the winter. You were smart
To have a poet as your servant in serious matters.
And what's more important than this closet on a string, the box that
Climbs vertically through the large, broken-down hotel, famous
For its spirits of bottled water! One of the two
Waiters finishing his smoke becomes careless . . .
There are screams of *Fire, Fire!* My faithless reader
Done with his sandwich, and a lover of big fires, returns
And says: *What an inferno, they are all lost; poor souls!*
I have not guessed the secrets of your closet. But out on the Atlantic

A ship bobs up and down, a sailor
Looks over to land and sees the burning parallax beams of the hotel.

The sailor's brow is like marble . . . my reader in a trembling voice
Speaks to the sailor, asking, "What's the matter, what's that
Fire on the shore?" The sailor answers,

"It's Hell, of course!"

THE WORLD ISN'T A WEDDING OF THE ARTISTS OF YESTERDAY

> *They were with me, and they were me . . .*
> *As we all moved forward in a consonance*
> * silent and moving,*
> *Seated and gazing,*
> *Along the beautiful river forever.*
> *   —Delmore Schwartz*

A stub of a red pencil in your hand.

A Georgia O'Keefe landscape rising beyond
The carcass of black larkspur,
Beyond the Milky Way where
The lights of galaxies are strung out over a dipper of gin
With a large sun and the rotund

Fuchsia moon. Her closet is empty, except for the manuscript
With your signature. She has left you!
Where was it in the field
That you threw the telephone:
After moving away
From the farmhouse, you found it again when
Returning for the lost cat—

As you walked through the low chinaberries calling
Her name you found the white horn
Of the telephone. You are alone calling to the frozen
Countryside of New Jersey.
She sleeps
In the yellow wicks of the meadow:
You are calling the mopsy cat back

From the ditch, but Dexedrine presses a pencil
Up against your eyebrow and temple. And
You've forgotten—*what was it?*

Out there in the field calling

Across the cold night air, drinking from the gold flask,
Again tucking that stub of a pencil
Back behind your ear. You read, this morning,
In the crisp pica lettering of the old Remington
How boatmen navigated the winter shallows of the Seine
Guided by a lamp burning all night
In a narrow window in Flaubert's study;

And all of a sudden, under severe stars, beside water,
You remembered everyone who was a friend.

But why your hand is locked on a red pencil, again,
At the bottom of a wintry meadow, in New Jersey,

Is a mystery rising behind you on the wind.

THE SCRIVENER'S ROSES

The gulls fly in close formation becoming a patch of sail . . .
They divide revealing a blue patch of sky. They dive
At a gun carriage on which the dead cot boy writhed
Much of last night. It is a flight of seagulls
Above the drying cannon brooms that makes the bay
Seem at all alive. It is over the dead water that the surgeons
Come:
                              over the bay American ships of war give up
Their cutters, the handsome surgeons climbing
Into rowboats and transported to the flagship where
The Surgeon of the Fleet chews patiently on beefsteak
Within this dark, dry
Man-of-War. They will gather for an amputation:
On dressers an orderly arranges saws and knives, sponges
And vials of iodine, the hooked darning needles are beside
The yellow bee's wax and thread. One boy is dead, another
Is barely alive. The oldest surgeon's face
Is white with scarlet brands like the ash hole in sickbay
With its few *live* red coals in a deep pan. The sawing on
The mahogany femur of the thigh is trying for the aging physician.
The leg will be hidden from sight behind a wood pile.
Across the bay on the beach a dark flamingo, in ridicule, stands
On just one leg. And a bugle signals
The return of the cutters to their separate ships.

The two dead boys are from New England. What had they endured?
They often said that an April snow was a poor man's manure.
Their sisters work in Carson's Old Paper Mill. The youngest girl
Worked a Tymer press, an iron machine that drops a weighted, sunken
Impression of roses onto a soft, scented stationery.
Two of the sisters have died in the mill, mauled by machinery!
The sleighs that are usually loaded with paper carried their bodies to
The cemetery on the hill.

Their distant cousin, Herman Melville, attended both burials.
He said to their mother, "Ruth, you still have a husband, two boys
At sea, and Elizabeth who'll soon marry. That Baker's stove
The girls gave to me flared up last week, scorching my study window.
The window now is like a Claude glass; it frames
The river and snowy fields
While giving them the golden lights of the Claude Lorrain landscape.
I'll remember the girls each time I stare through the panes
Of that almost amber window!"

Leaving his cousins, Melville on a train studies a passing meadow:
He has never before seen Jacks-in-the-pulpit flowering
In snow, standing in a late spring snow! He felt that the meadow
Was a white necropolis with toppled towers like halves of eggshells
After the weasel has raided the hen house.
He wondered if black ants were dead inside the walls
Of this wide, tufted city? He longed for the hearth.
For cider bottles popping in the cellar. For muffins with honey!

He will visit a small branch of The Dead Letter Office in Washington:
A large house with bare rooms, five rooms in the round, and
Each has a fireplace leading to a common, federal chimney. Five clerks
Wrapped in scarves stand before their assigned fire. They open
The letters spilling coins and rings into a steamer trunk. There are
The thin silver rings for children; rings of engagement for fingers already

Tattered to the bone like masts of a ghost ship under an opaque moon.
These letters
Spoke of affection, luck fishing for trout, of drought, of the deaths
Of this and that rich uncle. Five clerks at each fire, five fires! The black
Smoke rises from the single great stack, and a shopgirl across
The street in her attic room writes a letter describing
The smoke as it drifts
Out over Washington to the bay and woods. She writes
On scented sheets
To her brother who is at sea. He died in February. She is run over
That evening by a wagon loaded with raw cotton. Herman Melville stood

Over her in the street.
Just above her blue stocking, above
The blue garter
Is a wound in her thigh and a spurting artery, horse manure
And young active flies . . .

Walking back to the hotel he decides to return to his home by Friday,
He'll sit on the North porch and write and heal, the North porch
Like a sleety deck of a ship where the Captain is lashed to the wheel . . .

That Appius Claudius failed to drain the Pontine marshes is similar,
He believes, to this government's failure to burn all the dead letters
Of just a single week! He feels they could simply be scattered like gulls
                    from the crow's-nests of ships out on the open sea!

                                        *

The convent is in ruin. The churchyard is a basin filled with graves and
It extends into the adjacent park where farmers are chopping down trees
So as to be able to dig more graves late that evening. Sherman's artillery
Has destroyed the joists and center beam of
The convent, killing fifty-three nuns and an old priest. The farmers cut

Down trees and the birds and red squirrels are fleeing to the stream that
Is beside the old Saw Mill and its livery . . .
The next afternoon the Union soldiers enter the town,
They lose the light

Of day while looting and drinking. At dusk, searching for women, they
Arrive at the churchyard—with bayonets they open the fresh mounds
Where the sisters were hurriedly buried. Lanterns are strung up
In the few standing trees, the cook plays his red accordion, and
The men in their blue caps and jackets are dancing clumsily with
The dead women who have been stripped to the waist; their white bibs
And black birdcloth veils littering the green bowl
Of the dim churchyard:
Out of the mouths of the jostled corpses fall grave soil and
Ivory crowns from teeth. The dancing soldiers are laughing

With their rigid partners in moonlight—you can hear dry bones
Breaking! Some of the women are shaven, one has long red hair.
Their white breasts bouncing in the chill night air. Behind the hedge
Of the churchyard three black children hide while sobbing.
They understand these free men grinning through beards,
Drinking whiskey; one falling back into an empty grave.
Two sergeants, who are yet boys, are undressing the gray-haired
Mother Superior . . .

In this judgment the dead climb out of their shallow places
And waltz—all but three are now completely naked!
There are haloes of cigar smoke over the struggling couples.
The nun with red hair is young and freckled with a bloodless bayonet
Wound in her neck. One of her eyes is bruised shut; the other is
Open, ice-green and resigned. A bonfire is started.

You can hear hammers striking rail down by the depot.

The severe ebony and pearl garments of the sisters are thrown
On the fire. And what we know

Is that in the morning these soldiers, in a line three deep,
Moved on through Georgia for the sea . . .

*

The Chinese creeper climbing over lilac beside the piazza
Is infested with worms. The swing
On the piazza is nudged by wind, and Melville
Empties his pipe against the stone drain.
On the porch, at sunset, he trembles a little
Both in act and shadow,

Memento mori . . . the Antigone of paper, who dropped her sweet, iron
Roses onto thin polished sheets; but her sister, Elizabeth,
Is alive and has
Written from Washington to their brothers, the sailors;

They have been buried in a tropical cemetery for paupers and pilgrims.
Elizabeth has accidentally rented a room across
From the house to which her letter will be delivered.
She has told her brothers there will not be civil war.
She enclosed a watercolor miniature that depicts nuns bent in labor
In a sunny cotton field in Georgia.
And up the federal chimney goes this gesture of an ordinary, occult
Shopgirl. The genius of her vigil mixes ashes with ashes,
Tears with tears, and ink with the long white fabric of paper . . .

A fisherman
Out at sea held a packet of seeds and wished he'd hear
The madness of roosters as he neared the land and long beaches.
The winter beaches with their snowy dunes, white on white, or

Memento mori . . . the crisp depression of a clear rose
On its clear stem. This perfumed impression
In the corner of a crème paper
Is our lesson in understanding him: Melville dreamed he was

At sea in a state cabin which was sealed and caulked for an eternal
Crossing of the Atlantic. There are mice
In the desk drawers. Dust everywhere. And large linens
Draped over the furniture and mirrors.
It was like the mystery of an ancient scroll.
It was losing your soul down the awful mouth of a newborn, the perfect
Mouth spitting breast milk, while the infant in coarse swaddling
Is bricked up
                    inside the convent's south garden wall.

THE CIRCUS RINGMASTER'S APOLOGY
TO GOD

It is what we both knew in the sunlight of a restaurant's garden
As we drank too much and touched
While waiting for the lemon wedges and rainbow trout.
If it's about that door? I'm not sorry.
You smiled through tears. The night clerk said that I was
Crazy like a bear. Laughing, you spilled your beer.

Over the hedge a farmer paints a horse's cankers
With a heavy tincture of violet . . .

Later, in a dark room, both of us speckled, middle-aged, and soft.
I dragged my mouth like a snail's foot up your leg and body
To your mouth. We both shivered.
You ran naked before a window. Shyness increases your importance!

I don't know what you think when we are no one for a moment:
Hay-ropes, hands at ankles, gone beyond
Even the dripping faucet and its sink spilling onto the floor . . .

There's no strongbox hidden in the closet.

It's often like laughter, "You go pee for me and I'll boil the water."
Sipping hot coffee, you told me a story about the old ringmaster
On the Baltic shore:
                    he's inside his little house on wheels, and
The goldfinch jumps from its silver platform to the cage's floor that's
Littered with straw and shredded handbills. The ringmaster daydreams
About ponies circling in a white path of ashes . . .
On the table before him there's an ounce of tobacco
And in his plate: blue and gray parsnips, beef and the open letter

That he knows better than the loose floorboard! The two of us
Enjoy our solitude:
                    folded over chairs are the clothes

We never wore. If you die first, I'll sway in the hallway like a bear.
I'll whisper, "I'm sorry." And you'll
Not unlock the door.
I'll break through with my hip and shoulder . . .
Remember? You were glad that I did it once before!

COLERIDGE CROSSING THE PLAIN OF JARS

The gypsies carry sacks of walnuts out of the groves.
A dog
Whimpers below the cemetery, near to the peat field.

With regard to color primarily, but also
Scent and form,
The browsing deer under the sycamores
Have the very properties of a peach
Spoiled on the branch by a blanketing frost . . .

The deer, in Asia,
Rise out of fog as though it were a pond.

I walk. And over the wind, I hear the crushing
Of talc for the shaping of a death mask. Why is it?

Young Keats is lost!

Joseph Severn's hurried sketch of the rouged corpse
Was like that deep violet thumbprint, this morning,
In the soft breast of a goose
Hung in the draughty printshop of my publisher!

Sarah watched from her window above the philodendron
While I crossed against the West Wind
Through the drifting snow. She lost sight of me
For a moment. She guessed I was again wrestling
The angel.
I did die there, briefly, in the blizzard
As I had once with my mother as a boy—
The first of April, nude except for our canvas shoes,
We stepped
Under the bitter waterfall fed with a run-off of snow.

My brain empties

As it will when I've stood under the compass
Of a great low chandelier, weighted
In the purity
Of vertical tiers of burning citron candles.

The gypsies' bonfire climbs the stone face
Of the nunnery . . .
A Christmas pie, already sampled by the children,

Sits on the cleared table.
I stepped into the parlor, and Sarah said, "I thought
The elements had swallowed you
Just as you passed the last sycamore?"

She smiled in her chair, from half-dark,
And sewed—
I knew the chipped fire of pond ice
Was in her eyes like a widow's soul.

NOT THE CUCKOLD'S DREAM

He lifts the white skiff up onto the beach. It is Easter.
He hears the tin bells of the peninsula. A storm coming?
Two torches smudge, then,
In the blue night, burn cleanly again . . .
The pearl slapdash of the moon

Is on the water. He lifts a flying fish
By its pink underwing, hurriedly snipping
With his teeth the last bloodblisters
Like a string of peppers ripe across his fingers.

At the rope ladder, he pauses and sits on the cold sand
To rub life into his feet.
He rinses his infected hands in the fire of bound cat-tails.

The fisherman touches the ladder of maguey flesh, and
Pulls up!
Swaying, he is like a gull's shadow
Climbing on thermals before the white cliff. The tide

Will follow behind him, rising in a storm
It shatters the long skiff against the red adobe hen house.

His strong, dark wife, a giantess, thought it was personal.
She comes out waving, in hysteria, a handkerchief.
She loses her laughter to a stitch. The wind taken from her:

She is knocked back and then down
By the falling water. The heavy pleated dress

Washes over her ashen face. She wished
He had learned to swim.
There is a feeling of needles in her legs. He told

Her about the sea. *The sea is always feeding.*
The blood of his blistered hands is in his hair.
The fisherman raises dry bread to his mouth.

If I do not drown, *he thought of the father,*
I will marry, *he thought of the fish* . . .

V

NEW POEMS

AN OLD WOMAN'S VISION

No better day to come,
The breath of a worm-soft wind
Lifts me above the hill
Above the narrow road through pine barrens;
I smell father's flower,
The long blue valerians, they stood
In a round of dark inkweed
And bird foot violets. The old skunk,
Midnight, sometimes sat
In that loft of the garden,
Invisible in the stript light of the moon.

The visiting nurse said
My fever would spike after supper; the wind
Lifts and then drags fireflies
In white zig-zags, in a child's chalk,
Through night air. There's no chance,
In crossing,
That love will fail. I buried the cat,

Then blood showed in the pail.
A spider sits in his milk plate.
My cat with his snowy neck
Died with a blood blister
On his pink shaved hip and now that the smell
Of dirt is on him
Down in the yellowing underworld
Of bunchgrass, I fall back

And fly to where swamp gas
Rises to light the ditch to the old pond.
Here, all gooseflesh,
My husband waded through the reeds
Then to swim across to me:

The silk belly of a frog, he rose
From the bottom and broke the water
With a sound
Like a sucking stone going down . . .

SEVERAL MEASURES FOR
THE LITTLE LOST

The lesson begins in a heated room
Within a fortified wall of the old town;
Here, hundreds of years earlier, below the darkened window,
Two armies, one blue, one gold,
Crossed through each other in a ruin of mud, cries
Of fallen horses volleying
With muskets and cannon, waterfowl rising. . . .

But, now, the lesson has begun: the mother putting wood
In the porcelain stove,
Her child at the piano dreaming
Of the white charged wings
Of the constellation, *Cassiopeia*—
Last light striking
The oak and brass armillary beside the teacher
Who is eating from a cold leg of lamb.

There is the ordinary compass of a violin
Leaping from the left hand of the prodigy.
The teacher, this early spring,
Wonders why he is thinking
Of a pear-shaped mute of vellum
Being thrust into the bell of a trumpet.
He asks for more mustard on the lamb. The mother
Scurries into an adjoining room . . .

Equal spaces are being swept out in equal times!

The child is concentrating on the pedals
Moving beneath his trousers, saliva gathering
At the corners of his mouth
And his foot in its dark slipper
Raises the damper from the wire

/ 1 2 7

So that the final sound may be prolonged
After the child's finger has left the ivory key,
After all of the lamb has left the bone it warmed.

GRANDMOTHER

A spider floats from the apple tree
With a silk thread
Through air to the blossoming dogwood.
The long silk,

Spittle and linchpin, is cut
By the wing of an evening grosbeak.

Over the late lawn,
Between flowering trees like blue parallel snowfields,
Is a cedar birdhouse
Within which a man wakes. The cut thread,
A function of silence . . .

He rises in a renouncing space to a song:
A sharp, double *whit-sweet*.
The corn husks will serve as clothing.
The new light within him passes, incognito,
Down silk like a darkening hall:
In the hours he was visited:

The cloak of nearness, his dead grandmother,
Who speaks, "No more yellow wheat; joint of beef!"

He woke within cedar walls,
She stood beside him and he was quieted
As though no one
Had proved to be there at all.

PICTURES AT AN EXHIBITION

It's best, when watching the surprising levitations
Before the great gates of Kiev,
To believe the children are suddenly silent
Because an autumn storm,
                              still distant,
Announces itself through them—
                                          they go
To their separate meditations
Like sparrows down to the raw ditch.
The juggler's copper balls
                              are no longer
Gushing from his sleeves. Dwarves
Are climbing down from each other's shoulders:
The largest of these blue diminutives
                                          drops—
An afterthought making him roll
Before the wheels of a hurried cart:
On the other side
                    he springs to his feet, laughing
And the bells
Hooked on his ears are loudest
Now for him.
Two bearded priests
Stopped their spitting to watch
                              the dwarf's daring somersault.
Black thunderheads are over the eastern towers
Of the city. The grief
                        in this music repeats a dusky scene
For me. *For you I will see what I can see.*
An old troubadour and a red gnome with a damaged leg
Step with a lantern down from the casement
Leaving the catacombs:
                        beyond them the dark castle is barely
Visible in the heavy architectural waters:
                                          the skulls

Are somehow illuminated from within themselves. Why
Is it not possible for us to realize
That all
Of the skulls are grinning in this large generation
Of calcium and light.
                                    I am not sorry. I said
That for you
                    I will see what I can see: *all of the dead*
Are grinning!
It is not personal music that believes in *one* soul, or two
Twined

For or against mystery, *this is misery. . . .*
It is why you have left me
                                    with the most personal of beliefs
In the one and the many. Moussorgsky's friend, a painter, died
As we must to this and that life.
I will admit I am drinking tonight, hearing the promenade
Of the romantic Moussorgsky, ten notes
                                    crisp as the spade collars
Of the harassed nurses
                    with their charges in the Tuileries.
The children are set to quarreling, sparrows
Dropping to the ditch.
                              All these centuries
We have shared the storms, their beauty
Sweeping through the city, making of the one,
                                    the many.
I will admit the children have stopped quarreling
In the queer yellow light that felled the birds.
All motion is a little arc between two deaths. And if
You think you are justified by light
                                    then you have rolled
To your left shoulder, tucked your head,
Smelled,
          ever so briefly, the manure caked
To the huge insides of the thighs of oxen
Who are punished with a birch stick

By a farmer in flight
From the certain promise of rain,

                    the children strangely silent,
And up you come, again, as if sprung
From the toes
           that take the shock of your landing.
Rain splatters on your open face and hands. . . .
Music is everything!
                         I admit

The little fists of the dwarf opening in the air
Are reason enough to live,
                 reason enough for Moussorgsky to die
Less than ten years after his friend. I know
Nothing, virtually nothing of either of them.
                     But this

Is not the pattern the dwarf left in the air, *unbuckling*
What?
        All those large, fully formed organs
Inside his tiny frame. Maybe? Maybe just our fertile, giant need
To please ourselves,
             who are the many. It was another century,
                          haggling
We so reduce things! Do you see,
               with time,
How music is everything; even risk,
           set aside like land, will be blessed by rain.

TO A YOUNG WOMAN DYING AT WEIR

She hears a hermit laughing
Like a great scapegrace of waxwings and crows.
He is laughing about the burdock seed

That is in the horse manure
That is in the Sheriff's compost.
Last night, unable to sleep,
She recalled the catbird
Wheezing out in the chinaberry tree.
Soon frost would splatter
Iodine all over the hydrangeas
And the deer would no longer graze
Under the blood maples along the hill.

Sometimes her spirit grows and she remembers
A mountain dulcimer being played
While a woman sews. When the fear is largest
She remembers the old hermit poling his boat
Back along the cooling pond, he's taken burlap bags
Of the whitest sand from the cove
For plastering the walls of his autumn shack:
This comforts her,
                    errand and prospect,
A freshened sense of snow
Feathering over the frozen pond. She says
                    in a hush
That she loves something she has not found.

PENELOPE

I have looked for you at the familiar center
Of the turning red trees, a few
Alder leaves rising with lustrous
Sheets of rain that change
To green streamers like ivy darkening
The windowpanes. . . .

I have smoothed the earth over a suitor's grave.
The loom sleeps
Having eaten of the shorn path
That crosses under the belly of the lamb. . . .

Once you slept across me,
The big pulse in your thigh
Laid like a coin over the pulse that's down low
On my stomach;

The moon drags the sea
To the chalk shelf of red trees—
And I am bitter about everything, but

The radishes deliver themselves early
To please me; the hard
White peas are sweetening
Among fat mint leaves. The changing

Of the seasons has made sleep easy—
I have watched for the naked stranger, Ulysses,
Who in the dead thesis of voyage, avoids me.

CHEMIN DE FER

A chapel has fallen into ruins:
The still-standing corners, each with two
Gray triangles
Like stone bathers reclining
On their elbows along a white, windy shore . . .

This ruin in the meadow was the dominion
Of Francis of Assisi, who tamed
The large wolf. *He dreamt of an iron road*,
And was kind to the hour.
At noon, he said to the turtle

Whatever he had said earlier
To the difficult sparrows in the morning meadow.
He dreams
Of an iron cocoon nesting in fire,
And he was kind to the hour!

His chapel fell into flowers years ago:
Lilies of the valley: you know
That each has a white hood shaped
Like the spout on an old water pump—

Its severed goose wing of snow.

ELSINORE IN THE LATE ANCIENT AUTUMN

I hear a dead march. A thin wrist is mincing roses
In the diagonal lights of the castle's arbor.
It is the nun at her stone bench.
We need new quantities
Of perfume for our palpable dead!

The landlord is no longer at war. Someone whispers

To me, "Yorick? Yorick?"
There are four gates to the cemetery.
The North Gate opens to the Northwind.
The North Gate closes in the Southwind. As I lie awake,
Past midnight,
I can identify the prevailing wind
By its loud entrance into the churchyard:
According to the season, I can say
What future weather
Comes to Elsinore by calling
The cardinal sequences of gates—four compass points,
By eight voices that creak, each
With individual personality, in the night . . .

To the West, below the drawbridge,
The dew-mirrored vortices of wolfspiders
Are drying in anise weed.
The hourglass nest of a wolfspider
Was copied by me in willow and damask.
From this contrivance the fishermen
Made baskets which collect unguessed weights
Of flounder and sweet seabass.
Once, these men desired nothing more
Than the iridescent withers of a strong horse,
A few potatoes, and lasting benefice.

When the Prince's blue foot
Broke into cold space, all spectators went dumb!
The queen looked to me for strength:
Her Clown returned the anxious inquiry
By whispering, "My Dame, you've swallowed him, we think!"
She silenced me with her cold hand!

From a hanging tree the dressed stag in air
Swayed under a shifting weight of flies,
From the secret place I stole the gamekeeper's
Black wrap of knives. We opened Gertrude,
In the French manner, along her hairline—

There was a peal of ordinance
To announce our Prince, alive and strong! The King
Said a prayer from the checkered parapet
That commands the Sound.
Storied is the world, plotted is the ground.
That's what I sing to the sandy
Dog-pimpernels, in spring, in their new havens . . .

The night of Prince Hamlet's birth,
It was said,
Worms came up out of the earth
Without a promise of rain to summon them?
I upset the bowl of my warm breath
Over the newborn's mouth and nostrils.
He resented this, I laughed
While the Queen patted him dry with lambskin.

The nun, done chewing at the rosebuds, brought
In for me a cockleshell
To be worn in young Hamlet's hair.
This shell of a mussel is the badge for pilgrims
Bound to places of devotion
Beyond the sea—
In a day, old Fortinbras is defeated; the new Hamlet

Cries into this Fool's ear, and the pine weirs
Sank mysteriously into the North Sea . . .

Past three, still unable to sleep,
In disbelief I heard all four gates
To the churchyard
Opening and closing simultaneously—
Only a devil wind, undercut with wintry air,
Could visit us with such commotion! In the morning,
I was asked by Gertrude to speak of it . . .
I feigned madness that winter, not answering her,
And, in April, with the gray eyes of potatoes,

They buried me.

AT MIDSUMMER

For Jeannine

We had been in the tall grass for hours—
Sleep coming on some barrier of bells
Waking you—you stretched, the moon lost
In clouds, the gravestones below us
To the north had moved
West to a hill, the white rounded stones,
All at cruel angles to the ground,
Had been white and black heifers resting
Beside the stream with its ledges of quartz marl.

Earlier you had thought the stream
Moved like clear muscle and sinew
With their hooks
In the narrow runners of limestone.
You stretched, your breasts uncovered—
You had hurt your back lifting seed basins
Out in the shed; eased,
Touching me, you think of Kabir, saying:

Worlds are being told like beads.
The day began with the famous airs of a catbird,
A white unstruck music, you were downstairs
Sweeping mouse dirt out of the cupboards.
Now, down in the grass I am awake. I look over
To the north. And say: *It's gone? The gravestones?*
You smile and cross over me like a welcome storm.

PARISH

I.

God only knows what he'd been doing. Painting or sewing?
All I can say is that from my window
In the old yellow-and-black parsonage
I had been looking across falling snow
To the brick mortuary on the other side of the road.
It had one lamp burning; the mortician
Had thrown off his white gown, washed
His hands above the forearms, was exhausted,
And sat down. The water still running.

II.

I had a little friend once
Who fixed her own dolls: the walleyed, the lame,
And the gutted. She lived in a small town like this one.
She grew up to be odd.
All day I'd waited for a visitor
Who wasn't coming, all highways
Now closed by bad weather.

III.

He'd left the water running cold over porcelain.
He'd thrown down his gown. Looked out at the road.
Hypnotized by the snow and running water,
He gazed off to the body of hills.

IV.

The wind grew for some hours, then it was dawn.
The storm over. I could see footprints
That had shallowed with the drifting snow, that had
Come to our door in the dark—

Perhaps some transient
Looking for an early breakfast after a night
Of journeying and enchantment. I smelled
Dahlias—thoughts of Saint Jerome's lion
　　　Carrying a burden of wood in for the stove.
　　　I glanced
　　　To the footprints,
　　　Which had circled, waited; circled some more,
　　　And left our door, leaping the fence

　　　Or passing through it, all signs
　　　Of them vanishing into the hills.

REVELATIONS

—circa 1948

I.

I made no sound at all like the wintering
Of the paper wasp, or milch cattle
In fog,
Or the mud-caked winesaps in the cellar.
I just watched the neighbor
Up in the ladder with his torch.
The wooly nests of the tent caterpillars
Swelled as he sent them off with fire.
All that morning he poured Clorox
Down the anthill under the linden.
I read about children gone mad
With the shelling in Jerusalem.

It was two nights before
Charles Cobb stood outside his barn
And saw beyond the potatoes
A triangle of blue lights
Revolve above his firepond. The newspaper
Said it was *other beings,* and it spoke
Of war in the Holy Land. That night
The neighbor climbed into the elm again
With a torch. An hour passed,
Then he grabbed at his heart! He was there
Until morning in the big gnarled
Crotch of the tree. I slept in the window

Seeing in my dream the neighbor
Twenty years earlier, in a January thaw,
The flashpoint of his rifle in the pines,
Deer running out onto the pond, the ice
Breaking under them, just antlers

Thrashing above water like the dark bare
Branches of sumac that are there now.
A span of mules
Dragged the frozen deer up the winter road.

II.

Out of my mother's sleep I heard those light
Watery ovations in the spring onions.
I woke to watch the black ant
Milk the happy aphid right on the rose.
I listened to the hoarse *chack-chack*
Of the partridge working like the adze blade
In the woods. At dusk I looked up
At the hill, the caterpillars were spewing
Their gauze boxes again in the elm.
The neighbor's son was out to get them.

A whole year
The ladder had lain there on the ground.
The neighbor's boy walked it up
Into the tree, dipped his torch of rags
Into gasoline, and lit them. On the night breeze
A sleeve of fire drifted down behind him
And splattered on the lawn where the weight
Of the ladder's drowse had left its image
As dead grass which began to burn
Missing, like the ladder itself,
A high rung.
                    I watched. And made no sound . . .

ELEGY FOR WRIGHT & HUGO

Saint Jerome lived with a community
Of souls in a stone house.
He had a donkey and a young lion.
Winter evenings the brown donkey
Went out for wood, the proud lion
Always his faithful companion.

One night passing merchants seized
The donkey. The lion
Returned to the house
And was accused by Jerome
Of having eaten his friend!
The punishment was merciful—the lion
Assumed the donkey's burden
And went alone each winter evening
Across the fields
For firewood. The lion missed
The donkey, but he never
Felt wronged or misunderstood.

Years passed. And then
The merchants, with troubled conscience,
Detailing their shame, returned the donkey
To Saint Jerome.
The donkey and the lion
Resumed happily their winter schedules.
Everyone was forgiven. This is where
The story usually ends.

But months passed
And the lion, who missed his new usefulness,
Changed, became jealous, and snapped—
He ate the donkey under the stars
Among the cold alders.

He returned to the stone house
With a load of wood on his back.
Saint Jerome, not to be confused by experience,
Announced to the community
That the donkey was again lost,
That the lion had returned
With firewood, that the lion was bloody,
No doubt from combat, no doubt having attacked
The cruel merchants who had once again
Stolen his companion. But Jerome knew—
From then on the downcast lion
Was excused from all work, was left
To age by the fire.

Jerome, dressed in sack,
Went out each night
Barefoot across the blue snow
And returned with branches
Tied to his back.

He was a saint. It was like that. . . .

A NOTE ON THE AUTHOR

Norman Dubie was born in Barre, Vermont, in April 1945. His poems have appeared in many magazines, including *The Paris Review*, *The New Yorker*, *The American Poetry Review*, *Antaeus*, *The Antioch Review*, *The Georgia Review*, and *Poetry*. For his work, he has won the Bess Hokin Award of *Poetry* and a fellowship from the John Simon Guggenheim Memorial Foundation. He lives in Tempe, Arizona, with his wife and daughter, and is a member of the English Department at Arizona State University.